CERTIFICACIÓN DE PASO (sello)

En las casillas deberá figurar el **sello de cada localidad (al menos 2 por día)**
con la **fecha**, para acreditar su paso

FÁBRICA DA CATEDRAL DO PORTO †

Fecha

CAFÉ CJ'S

Caminho de Santiago

Rua da Ponte d'Ave, 184
Vilarinho - Macieira da Maia

Fecha

pedra furada
Café restaurante
Rua Santa Leocália 1415
4755-392 Pedra Furada
Tel.: 252951144
Barcelos

Fecha 10.07.2017

SRª. LªPA
P A S T E L A R I A
Pedro Manuel Azevedo Pires
NIF: 217 009 654
Rua Nª Srª Lapa 1290 - Aborim

Fecha 11-07.2017

Quinta S. Miguel de Arco
TURISMO RURAL
António José Rodrigues
Contribuinte n.º 614090001
Rua da Lavra, 209 — 4480-018 ARCO
VILA DO CONDE — Telef. Fax 252652...

Fecha 09/07/17

GARDEN
Barcelos

Fecha 10/07/2017

Residéncial Pinheiro Manso
De: João Maria Corrê...
Lugar Nab...

Fecha

CERTIFICACIÓN DE PASO (sellos)

En las casillas deberá figurar el **sello de cada localidad (al menos 2 por día)** con la fecha, para acreditar su paso

Residéncial Pinheiro Manso
De: João Maria Correia de Sousa
Lugar Nabais - Seara · P. Lima
Cont. Nº 147 760 933

Fecha 12 / 07 / 2017

NO LLEGA ANTES
EL QUE VA
MÁS RÁPIDO
SINO EL QUE SABE
Fecha DÓNDE VA

HOTEL IMPÉRIO DO NORTE
UNIPESSOAL, LDA
CONTRIBUINTE N.º 513 637 729
RUA 5 DE OUTUBRO, N.º 97
4990-030 PONTE DE LIMA

Fecha 12 / 07 / 2017

Fecha

Casa da Capela

13/07/2017

Fecha

Fecha

GOMES & BARROS, LDA
Rua de Oliveira
VALENÇA
Cont. N.º 504 222 880

14/07/17

Fecha

Fecha

CERTIFICACIÓN DE PASO (sellos)

En las casillas deberá figurar el **sello de cada localidad (al menos 2 por día)** con la fecha, para acreditar su paso

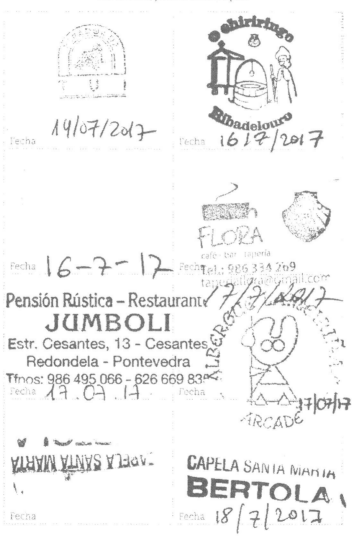

Fecha 14/07/2017

Fecha 16/7/2017

Fecha 16-7-17

FLORA
café · bar · tapería
Tel.: 986 334 209
taperiaflora@gmail.com
Fecha 17/7/2017

Pensión Rústica – Restaurante
JUMBOLI
Estr. Cesantes, 13 - Cesantes
Redondela - Pontevedra
Tfnos: 986 495 066 - 626 669 830
Fecha 17.07.17

ARCADE
Fecha 17/07/17

TAPELA SANTA MARTA
Fecha

CAPELA SANTA MARTA
BERTOLA
Fecha 18/7/2017

Northward to Santiago

To Dave

A rather plodding tale,
I fear. Just take it
step by step.
With all good wishes

Paul

Northward to Santiago

A curmudgeon on the Camino Portugués

PATRICK TIERNEY

First published 2020 by Cottage Grove Editions
Copyright © 2020 Patrick Tierney
'Poems' by Frances Hamblin first published 2018
Copyright © Estate of Frances Hamblin

A catalogue record for this book is available from the British Library.

ISBN 978-1-8380943-0-0
northwardtosantiago@gmail.com
Book design: Stone Creative
Cover Design: Version One
Printed by Kindle Direct Publishing

For Frances,
my shade along the way

Contents

Introduction 1

Map 5

Overture 7

Movements I 9

Frances Farewell 101

Movements II 105

Finale 223

Epilogue I: Poems for Frances 227

Stones in Our Pathway 229

Parting II 230

Grave Matters 232

Grammar Lesson 234

Pillow Talk 235

Touchstones 236

Epilogue II: Poems by Frances Hamblin 239

Editor's note 241

Star Travelling 243

Steroid Sisters 244

The Silver Birch 245

Mantequilla 246

Sandbanks, August 2011 247

Winter Reflections 248

Fucking February 249

Little Mote Song 250

Titanium Screws Blues 251

Let Me Go And The Music Will Flow 253

I Don't Cry 254

What Do I Wish For You? 255

Little Poem To My Grandchildren 257

I Am Not 258

Biographical note 259

Acknowledgements 261

Introduction

I felt like an imposter. In fact, I was an imposter. I was standing in the passenger terminal at Porto airport, dressed head to toe in dark sportswear and with a 44-litre rucksack strapped to my back. I looked and felt like a trussed-up turkey.

I was about to start walking the northern half of the *Camino Portugués*. This is one of the traditional routes that, for centuries, have drawn pilgrims to the shrine of the martyred apostle St James in the cathedral at Santiago de Compostela in northwest Spain.

As a firmly lapsed Irish Catholic, I certainly wasn't seeking spiritual benefit from the walk, but I had visited Santiago in 1994 and been charmed by the place. Since then, thoughts of tackling a Camino had occasionally popped into my head, but I viewed it purely as a physical challenge with the added benefit of an interesting, historic destination. Now, in the summer of 2017 a fortuitous family get-together in Porto had finally provided the opportunity to give it a try.

Over the next two weeks I would cover about 230 km (143 miles), with a day off in the middle. Such a distance, I knew, wouldn't raise a blister on the hardened feet of genuine hikers: veterans, perhaps, of the 630-mile roller coaster that is England's South West Coast Path or the even more inhuman achievements of through hikers on North America's legendary Appalachian or Pacific Crest Trails.

I was no such iron-shinned yomper. In the soft rolling downs of the south of England where I lived, I was a modest day hiker, happy with gentle rambles over well-groomed, carefully tended countryside that ended with a benediction of ale in a comfortable country pub. Not once in my 65 years had I walked for two full days in a row – never mind the two weeks I was now facing. And I had never shouldered a full-size rucksack. So, unsurprisingly, I was feeling slightly apprehensive and more than a few degrees south of my comfort zone.

My clothing didn't help. I am an old-fashioned cotton, linen and leather man. I wouldn't be seen dead in a polyester shroud. Yet here I was, dressed in an ultralight Rab top and multi-pocketed Ayacucho shorts. My feet were shod in light Hoka Challenger running shoes, in a particularly garish black and yellow 'colourway', as I believe one has to express it. The intimate details of my hi-tech, anti-chafing Swiss underpants I will reserve to a later chapter when we know each other better.

But, as I would be walking in the heat of the Portuguese summer, two friends – both experienced Camino walkers – had persuaded me to forsake all natural fibres and cling only to lightweight, wicking, quick-drying sports gear of the most artificial kind. I didn't know it then, but I would soon be very grateful that I took their advice. But at that moment, in all honesty, I would have felt more at ease in a burka.

I had just spent a few pleasant days with three of my four siblings in the hospitable ambience of Porto. With one brother based in Australia, one in Switzerland and my sisters and I sprinkled across Ireland and England, these get-togethers were rare and appreciated all the more as we grew older.

My own life was in a state of transition. It was less than a year since Frances, my wife and life partner of almost 43 years, had died as a result of a brain tumour. For the last years of her life, I had been her carer – the hardest and most intensive job I had ever done. I was still coming to terms with my unsought status as the first widower among my siblings and friends. Perhaps two weeks of solitary walking would help me process some of what Frances and I had endured together through those tough years and the life I now faced on my own.

As I waddled towards the terminal exit, I was at least glad that Frances had been spared the sight of her husband as a polyester Paddy. She had had her own strong views on most things, including what one should or should not be seen wearing in public. But this was not the moment to revisit the trauma of my brown 1970s Crimplene jacket. For now, my costume was donned; my role defined.

'*Vesti la giubba.*'

It was time to turn my back on the sun and head north.

Santiago de Compostela
Parada de Francos
Padrón
Caldas de Reis
Pontevedra
Arcade

SPAIN

Porriño
Tui
Valença
Casa Capela
Pinheiro   Ponte de Lima
Manso

PORTUGAL

Barcelos
Villa d'Arcos
Airport
Porto

.... International border
– – –   Camino Portugués

Overture

A molten full moon hung over Porto, turning the Douro into a literal manifestation of its name: the river of gold. From our apartment beside the cathedral, we could look beyond the graceful arc of the Dom Luís I bridge to the Port lodges lining the opposite bank. In Vila Nova de Gaia and all along the Porto side, the sounds of revellers drifted up on the warm July air. The weekend stag and hen parties were in town.

It was our last night in the city and we had finally found a restaurant that served grilled sardines – a prospect that made my sister very happy. It was a rough and ready locals' place in the otherwise touristy Ribeira district and, though my brother was initially sniffy (the restaurant, he said, had been awarded two Michelin tyres – rather a good remark I thought, if it was original), he eventually seemed to enjoy the honesty of the experience.

Later, after a couple of tawny Ports at a bar where our party of four raised the average age by at least a couple of decades, my sister and I said goodbye to our brother and his wife. Tomorrow they were setting off on a cruise of the Douro valley. They would, I was sure, quickly re-adapt to luxury.

Back at our apartment, we mopped up any wine left over from our four-day get-together and then retired to our rooms. For perhaps the tenth time that day I fussed over my rucksack, selecting items to keep handy near the top, while optimistically consigning rain gear to the depths.

Loud music still throbbed along the riverfront but, magically, just before midnight, the city fell silent. The kind people of Porto were doing their best to let me have a decent night's sleep before my Sunday resurrection as a pilgrim on the well-trodden path to Santiago.

Movements I

Porto to Tui

Sunday 9 July

Porto to Arcos

I looked left. I looked right. I glanced out the rear window. No one was about. Excellent. I leapt out of the taxi, grabbed my rucksack and walking poles and impatiently waved the driver on his way.

I had just come from Porto airport, where I had said goodbye to my sister who was catching a flight home to Belfast. Now I was standing by the side of the N306, a minor road winding out of the city towards the town of Vilarinho, but, more importantly, at this point, the route followed by the *Camino Português* heading north to Santiago.

I strapped on my rucksack, gratified that no one was around to see me shoulder it in earnest for the first time. I felt uneasy about skipping the long trudge out from the traditional starting point of Porto cathedral. But, as John Brierley, guru of all things Camino, points out in his guidebook, many *peregrinos* starting from Porto spare themselves the dull initial hike through busy main streets, soulless suburbs and warehouse wildernesses by simply taking the Metro to the edge of the city.

A swift taxi ride from the airport, round a small arc of the ring road, had much the same effect. I had no illusions or compulsion about being a completist on this hike. I was happy – if slightly abashed – to be numbered among the shirkers. And, anyway, I had saved myself 18 kilometres of unforgiving urban pavement.

Just as I was about to start walking, a rough-looking character, who had the air of someone who could well have slept in a doorway on the way out from Porto, wished me my first *'Bom Caminho'* – the greeting constantly exchanged by pilgrims along the Way. In Portugal it's *'Bom Caminho'* and in Spain *'Buen Camino'*. He was also toting a rucksack and continued striding purposefully northward. Happy to greet my first fellow pilgrim, I stuttered an ill-rehearsed reply then busied myself with various tasks and bits of equipment – applying sun lotion, donning sunglasses, pulling on my hat, extending my walking poles and finding room for the Camino guide in one of the many pockets with which my shorts were supplied. Finally ready, I took my first step.

The N306 may have been a quiet, minor road, but cars passed at surprising speed. I hadn't gone far before I met the rough-looking character walking back towards the city, looking no less purposeful than before. Clearly this was no pilgrim or perhaps he had thought better of the enterprise. Maybe he was a local who just prowled the Camino daily to check out the talent. In any case, I would have to be more circumspect and not simply assume that anyone else on the road would be shadowing me to Santiago.

A kilometre or so further on I fell in behind three Frenchmen: one older man accompanied by two younger lads. Two were lavishly tattooed and the older one, like me, used walking poles. He had a large Camino de Santiago badge stitched to the back of his rucksack, leaving little doubt that here were serious pilgrims. As we were all walking at much the same pace, I followed close behind for a few kilometres. We didn't speak, though one of the younger lads smiled back at me once to at least acknowledge my presence. It was clear, however, that this was a closed brotherhood.

The older man had obviously taken a vow to talk at least 10,000 words for each kilometre walked. He rabbitted incessantly about I know not what while his companions nodded and grunted in clear acceptance of the wisdom bestowed on him by his years.

I paced behind until we arrived at a *'deviso'* – a deviation, where a sign recommended taking a longer detour rather than proceeding straight along the N306 which, rather alarmingly, was now flagged up as a 'dangerous path'.

After a brief consultation with a passing local, the Gallic trio ignored the sign and carried straight on along the road. I set out to follow the deviation. It would, I thought, be a way of putting some distance between us and affording respite from Monsieur's ceaseless babble. I hadn't gone very far when a passing cyclist stopped me. Showing me a navigation app on a mobile phone strapped to his handlebars, he went to great lengths to explain the additional distance I faced if I followed the detour. As I had just started out and was somewhat unsure of my capacity for mileage on a sustained daily basis, I allowed myself to be persuaded to take the shorter route. With some misgivings I turned back and resumed the main road – a decision I quickly came to regret.

The road had become twisty and cars shot towards me at what seemed great speed and, though none came too close, I found myself approaching each blind bend with trepidation, ears straining for the sound of engines. To maximise sight lines on the all-too-frequent curves, I scuttled constantly from one side of the road to the other. All this edginess and dashing to and fro rather spoiled what I had envisaged would be a relaxing start to my Camino.

Still on the road, I marched through the tiny settlements of Mindela and Vidal and eventually came to a busy crossroads. This was the town of Vilarinho where a Sunday morning car boot sale was in full spate, with venerable relics of childhood, work and leisure on display. Old sewing machines and radios, farm tools and well-chewed toys were laid out to tempt a straggle of would-be buyers who were showing very little interest.

The charms of car boot sales have always eluded me and it still amazes me what people consider marketable. One person's junk is another's bargain find. In recent years, the growth of eBay and similar facilitators of recycled ownership seems to have kept a sizeable chunk of the western economy afloat, simply by regurgitating and revaluing previously digested items. We have eased sluggishly into the large intestine of the economic cycle. Who dared say what lay ahead?

By now the sun had come out and the atmosphere was warming up. Preserving my car boot virginity with very little effort, I carried on past the nondescript stalls and dropped into Café CJ's, the first bar of my Camino, for a welcome beer. Eyeing my rucksack and poles and clearly assessing me as a pukka pilgrim, the friendly host offered to put the first stamp in my unsullied *Credencial* which I had purchased for two euros in Porto Cathedral a few days earlier.

For genuine pilgrims, the *Credencial* is an important document. Each day hikers are required to have one or – for the crucial final 100 km – two dated stamps added en route. On reaching Santiago, the stamps provide a continuous log of their journey, proving they actually walked the Camino rather than taking a bus or taxi. In return, they receive a *Compostela*, a certificate that acknowledges their achievement in completing the pilgrimage.

Clearly impressed by the time I had made in reaching Valarinho, the barman asked if I had set out from the centre of Porto that morning. When I admitted that I hadn't actually walked out from Porto but from the *aeroporto*, he promptly accused me of cheating. But it was all in good humour and so, deserved or not, the first scallop shell of my journey was carefully inked in the space below the official cathedral stamp.

Thirst temporarily slaked and my first stamp safely in place, I continued on my way, delighted with the discovery that licensed premises were acceptable places in which to have my *Credencial* officially endorsed. What a blessing not to have to hunt down elusive priests, nuns or sacristans in sleepy ecclesiastical outposts along the way.

Beyond Vilharinho, after crossing a beautiful medieval bridge over the river Ave, the route finally veered off-road through quiet wooded byways. This was more what I had expected from the Camino. The path followed gentle uphill rises through quiet, restful countryside. All was deeply rural and idyllic. The day had become really hot and I was grateful for my lightweight sun hat whose wide brim protected my delicate Celtic ear tips.

Having learned from my earlier mistake, when a new detour was offered I turned off without question. It led me along dry earth tracks through densely planted fields where stately maize plants formed green walls on either side, blocking out the landscape. Eventually the path to Arcos, my destination for the day, resumed along traffic-free rural lanes. The day grew hotter and the countryside was sunk in Sunday slumber. With no one else around, I had the Camino to myself. At one point, just after I'd taken a welcome slug from my water bottle, I came across an office water cooler that a kind family had set up at the gate to their property. A notice told passers-by to help themselves and not leave any money.

As I walked along, Frances, my lost love, was very much in my thoughts. Of all the people I knew, I would have picked Frances as the least likely to die prematurely. She was energetic, full of life and – unlike me – open and accepting to people and experience. And, also unlike me, she took care of her body. I was more likely to vote Conservative than take out gym membership; Frances cycled almost daily and had practised yoga to a high level for years and, more latterly, Pilates. In all our time together she had had no major health problems.

All that changed utterly on 22 June 2010 when, completely unheralded, a glioblastoma grade IV – the most aggressive form of malignant brain tumour – was discovered. Frances was just 55 at the time.

Had we both managed to retire in good health, the Camino was exactly the sort of venture we would have set out on together. We had enjoyed many day walks and, just weeks before Frances's tumour was diagnosed, had even wandered a couple of short stretches of Hadrian's Wall in the North of England. But, as my father used to say: 'Do you know how to make God laugh? Tell him your plans'.

Now, walking alone, I found myself talking to her, telling her what I was experiencing and how much I regretted not having her by my side. What would have been her 63rd birthday was just weeks away, with the first anniversary of her death 22 days later. Almost a whole year had passed – a year of firsts, as so many people had told me: my first birthday as a widower; our first family Christmas and New Year without her; my first solo wedding anniversary. And, of course, our children's first birthdays without their mother. Frances loved celebrations and had put particular store on birthdays. Every year, since the children had been very young, she had created magnificent, sculptural cakes for their parties. Now, without her, all these annual milestones were fundamentally changed and diminished.

During the months since Frances's death and despite the wise counsel of family and friends, aspects of grieving had taken me by surprise. Well-meaning people had warned me that I might find the reality of her death hard to comprehend. Convinced of my profound rationality, I had dismissed their fears but they proved all too accurate. At times, in the weeks immediately after her death, I felt the whole thing had been a dreadful mistake: that somehow Frances might reappear, just walk back into the room as if she had been delayed somewhere. The sheer finality of the event – the irrevocable nature of the separation – was difficult to comprehend, never mind accept.

Sometimes, at home, if I dozed off in front of the television, I'd be astonished to wake up and find myself alone in the room. Where on earth was Frances? A particular moment, just when we were about to leave the graveyard after her funeral, stuck in my mind. Having checked that our children were all in the car, I stepped back to look for Frances. Where could she be? The realisation that she was not coming with us – that we had just had her funeral and left her lying in a newly dug grave – hit me with the power of a punch.

Then there was the terrible fear that maybe she hadn't actually been dead. Had she perhaps just fallen into a very deep coma? My God, had we buried her alive? This craziness wasn't helped when, some days after the funeral, I visited her grave. A combination of varifocal lenses and tear-misted eyes made it seem as though the broken earth was moving gently up and down, inhaling and exhaling.

Frances had been buried in a basketwork coffin in a natural burial site and, in subsequent weeks, as her grave settled and sank, some lines of Gerard Manley Hopkins, unthought of since university days, popped into my head:

The cold whip-adder unespied
With wavèd passes there shall glide
Too near thee, and thou must abide
The ringèd blindworm hard beside.

With time, of course, the angst and irrationality subsided, but a huge void remained in my life. In my 65 years I had never lived alone. In fact I hadn't even been alone in the womb: I have a twin sister, so, from birth, our lives were totally intertwined. I grew up with four siblings in an extended Irish family that embraced dozens of cousins and more than a few second cousins. I spent five of my early teenage years as a boarder in a harsh Catholic school where opportunities to be alone were fervently discouraged. Four years of communal student life followed at Queen's University in Belfast, with all the frantic sociability that entailed. This was where Frances entered my life.

In October 1973 Frances flew into Belfast for the first time, arriving from Cyprus where her parents were then living. She had spent the previous year on that sun-kissed island, allegedly polishing up a couple of A Levels in order to secure entry to university but, in reality, filling her days with swimming, sailing, sunbathing and attending as many cocktail parties as she could. She had arrived to read Philosophy and was determined to have a damned good time over the next four years. She had just turned 19.

Despite being a fairly late arrival for the year, with her typical good fortune, Frances was allocated a room in the only female hall on the university's complex of residential tower blocks. On the evening of her second full day in Ireland, she set out to explore the facilities the site offered.

At the time I was a third year student, still living in halls and very involved in a group that organised a weekly disco on site. That evening I was working in the upper function room, carrying out a complicated electrical repair on a piece of disco equipment – I was changing a plug.

The door burst open and in walked this tall, blonde, suntanned, open-faced, smiling creature. She was wearing a tight-fitting green top, a broad, orange suede belt and a short, grey, suede skirt that buttoned down the front. Her long, suntanned legs finished in a pair of wedge clogs, adding to her already impressive height. In the grim, grey, murderous city that was Belfast at the height of the Troubles, this was an exotic vision indeed.

We got talking and I persuaded her to come with me to one of the male halls to slide leaflets under the bedroom doors, advertising the first disco of the year which was due to take place the following Saturday. Right from the start we were a good team. We began at the top of the 10-storey block: one of us took the even floors, the other the odd and we met again on the ground floor. I then invited her back to my room and she agreed.

At the time I considered myself a sophisticated man of the world – at least in my own eyes. I had just returned from a summer working in New York City and had brought back two precious items of duty-free: a bottle of Cognac and a bottle of whiskey. Frances opted for brandy so I poured her a generous measure and then asked if she would like anything else. She turned to me, flashing the big, toothy, open smile with which I would soon become so familiar, and said: 'Some ice would be nice'. And that was it. We were together from that day for the next almost 43 years.

On the face of it, we were an unlikely pairing. I came from a hard-faced little town that possessed almost as many Presbyterian churches of various sects as pubs. The sort of place where, in the early days of the civil rights campaign in Northern Ireland, I had watched the loud-mouthed demagogue Ian Paisley carried shoulder-high through the streets by cheering supporters – the sort of people who were determined to forestall any such outrage to Ulster as 'one man, one vote'.

I had grown up in a grimly pious Catholic household where, on Sundays when we took communion, our father would insist on us attending chapel three times – for first and last Mass in the morning followed by a dull half hour of devotions in the evening.

My family – at least on my father's side – were committed teetotallers, proudly sporting Pioneer Total Abstinence Society badges on their lapels. Among such people, the choice of brown lemonade instead of white with Sunday lunch could be considered a bit risqué. Before arriving at university, my entire education had taken place in just two schools and, at the age of

22, the sum total of my foreign travel had encompassed only parts of England, New York and New Jersey.

Frances was a confident, outgoing English girl, the product of a very different and more liberal upbringing. Hers had been a peripatetic and occasionally exotic childhood – she quickly learned how easily she could rile me by referring to herself as 'cosmopolitan' in contrast to my bogwater-soaked roots.

She had been born in London but, just a few years later, sailed with her family for the horn of Africa where her father, a restless civil servant who pursued overseas postings whenever he could, had taken a position with the Colonial Office. So Frances's first experience of school was in an Empire outpost in the dusty heat of Somaliland. The smells, colours and sounds of Africa were to leave an indelible imprint on her.

Further stints of government-funded foreign living followed in Malta and Cyrus, interspersed with periods of 'normal' British schooling in the Home Counties and the north of England. By the time the mosaic of her education was complete, Frances reckoned she had attended no fewer than 13 different schools.

Whatever this shuffling between exam boards may have cost her in terms of stability or depth of learning, all those years spent ingratiating herself into strange classrooms and playgrounds had made her an excellent social mixer – someone with charm, empathy and people skills that I could only look upon with envy.

In contrast to my teetotal upbringing, Frances was a veteran of gin and tonic marathons in officers' messes in Malta and Cyprus. These were interspersed with flowing liquid receptions for visiting Royal Navy ships and carefree teenage party nights of kebabs and Kokinelli – a potent Port-like Cypriot wine – under starry Mediterranean skies.

But whatever the differences in our backgrounds, we quickly formed a strong, loving and equal partnership. We were a very close couple so it was hardly surprising that, through all our decades together, snatches of solitude had been few and brief. Now, days of solitude were mine for the taking on this two-week hike. They offered me space in which I might finally fully comprehend my loss and reconcile myself to the new life to which I was gradually adapting. I may have been only a few miles into my hike but in my head I knew: Frances would be walking the Camino with me. This would be our last journey together before going our separate ways: she into the mists of memory and I to a future yet to be shaped.

But why the Camino? There were plenty of other trails that could offer solitude and physical challenge without the dried spittle of sanctity and the encrustations of belief that clung to the Camino. I had absolutely no religious or spiritual motivation for my walk. True, I had been brought up as a member of what the poet Patrick Kavanagh called Ireland's 'prayer-locked multitude'. I had emerged from a particularly joyless form of Ulster Catholicism – the sort that competed with an equally grim Ulster Presbyterianism to see who could achieve greater misery in this life, the better to inherit glory in the next.

I had been an earnest, credulous child and, of course, utterly brainwashed into believing that to be baptised a Catholic was to receive the greatest gift of all. Despite our Protestant fellow citizens ostentatiously chaining up swings and roping planks on to playground slides in the parks on Sundays – after all, nothing remotely pleasurable could be allowed to distract even toddlers from a Sabbath spent poring over the Good Book – we Catholics alone enjoyed the blessing of 'the one true faith'. And how often did we hear that phrase?

I took it all on board with barely a whimper, but, when I learned about Limbo, some incipient rationality caused me to begin to question and even regret my baptism. Limbo was a unique place which harboured the souls of babies who died before they could be baptised. Among my tribe this was considered an immense tragedy but, of course, it was kind of God to set aside a special place for the poor wee things. And Limbo offered, we were assured, all the delights of Heaven –

but without that greatest reward: the sight of God. What? All that eternal happiness but without the harp-playing, the hymn-singing and the endless praising of the 'Big Fella'? The lucky sods. I'd settle for that.

Then, somewhere along the way – long after I'd stopped caring – Limbo was abolished. So where were all those deprived wains now? Probably in a remedial music class in some out-of-the-way celestial ghetto. For all I knew, Purgatory and Hell were next for the chop – or perhaps they'd already gone. After all, if you believed the traditionalists, every time the current Pope opened his mouth, another chunk of masonry fell from the dome of St Peter's and smashed into the marble below.

After wrestling my way out of conventional religion, the meretricious glibness of new age spiritual wafflery held no attractions. But I must confess (loaded word) I retained many of the cultural accretions that come with Christianity. I loved church architecture – the older the better. Solid, unadorned Romanesque churches were particular favourites. The *Camino Francés*, the most important of the traditional pilgrim routes to Santiago, which runs from the Pyrenees westward along northern Spain, was blessed (!) with many fine examples; not so much the *Portugués*, I suspected.

I'd grown up among the pastiche gothic of the garish parish churches that were flung up all over Ireland following

Catholic emancipation in the 19th century. This made genuinely ancient buildings all the more attractive – sometimes in a comically poignant way. It amused me when, visiting a venerable English parish church – Anglican, of course – my father would stare at the beauty around him and sigh: 'Was this one of ours?' It was as though, in some post-reformation settlement, a penitent Church of England might one day do the decent thing and 'we' would get some of the good stuff back. I was never sure if my father was being serious or ironic. I suspect the former: it was more his way.

Another aspect of my religious heritage that remained strong despite my apostasy was a delight in liturgical and choral music. But, when it came to religious art, I could sustain my interest only so far: in galleries like the Uffizi and the Louvre, I would hit peak 'Madonna and Child' very quickly. But, in tune with my passion for opera, I retained a tolerance of or perhaps even a taste for the theatricality of ritual. The bells, the incense, the singing of the *'Te Deum'* at the end of the first act of Puccini's 'Tosca' were guaranteed to have the hairs on the back of my neck springing upright.

I understood the tribal need for pomp and ceremony at important moments in a community's shared existence and, after two millennia of practice, the Church was more than adept at stage-managing such occasions.

Following Frances's death I had had to confront my own dilemma on this score. An extremely popular woman, Frances had wide circles of friends from various areas of her life that overlapped and interlocked like the rings of the Olympic logo. For her funeral I needed to find an adequate space to accommodate the large number of people I thought might attend. Frances had chosen burial rather than cremation, but would have rejected a normal church funeral service – not least because she was a non-believer but she particularly despised the lugubrious sing-song delivery preferred by so many Anglican clergy. So the options were limited. If one rules out crematorium and church, few sizeable spaces remain that could host a secular funeral service – or at least that was the case in our home city. And this is a problem that, I think, will only become more pronounced as unbelieving baby boomers start to fall off the perch in numbers.

In my head I had a preferred location: the ancient church of St Thomas à Beckett which stands at the head of Chichester Harbour and just next to the green burial site where Frances would be interred. But this was an Anglican church, so how could we possibly hold a secular funeral there without, as they say, 'benefit of clergy'? One of Frances's best friends – a committed Catholic, as it happened – suggested there was nothing to lose by making an inquiry. The Church of England, she said, sometimes made its buildings available for purposes other than parish worship.

So I contacted the verger in charge of funerals (helpfully identified on the church's website) and explained my case. He didn't dismiss me out of hand but made it clear he would require 'some reference to a higher power' in whatever service we were planning. I explained we would be singing Blake's 'Jerusalem', one of Frances's favourite hymns from her schooldays. That pleased him, but he suggested we might also like to recite something along the lines of the Lord's Prayer.

I agonised for all of an instant. Frances – a beneficiary of what we Catholics would have dismissed as a lax Church of England heritage – was much more pragmatic in these matters than I. At baptisms, weddings and funerals of various denominations, she would join in enthusiastically with the hymn singing and ritual. Such communal religious observance raised no issues for her. I knew Frances would not have objected to the Lord's Prayer, so I agreed to the verger's conditions. And, in return, we would be able to host our own funeral rite for her in a soothing, hallowed space – a place that had been revered and treasured since Saxon times.

I quickly informed family and friends that we had a date and venue for the funeral. But things took an unnerving turn when, three days beforehand, I visited the church to meet the lady in charge of the flower arrangements. Noticing a bearded man busying himself about the sanctuary, I was informed he was the verger and decided to introduce myself. He immediately launched into an explanation as to 'the procedure we adopt when there isn't a coffin'.

Somewhat taken aback, I said: 'But there will be a coffin'.

'There will be a coffin? But this is a memorial service, isn't it?'

'No. This is my wife's funeral. As I explained, she is being buried in the green burial site alongside and I contacted you to ask if we could hold her funeral service here.'

Clearly flustered, the verger mumbled something about needing to consult his notes. We walked to the back of the church where he began to thumb through a large, black diary while I stood, rictus-faced, thinking: 'Holy Christ, he's not going to pull the rug from under me just three days before the funeral.'

Never mind that friends and family from Ireland and Scotland had already booked flights, I was under a pressing time constraint. My younger daughter Hannah's wedding was due to take place the following week and I didn't want that event to be dominated by commiserations for her mother's sad demise. In my view it was imperative that the funeral should be behind us before Hannah's big day. But arranging a funeral in

England is not a speedy affair: it invariably takes weeks. It's a much more rapid business in Ireland where you're in the ground a mere two days after the ink has dried on your death certificate. I had somehow managed to organise Frances's funeral for just 12 days after her death, but was that all about to crumble?

Eventually, after much flicking of pages and nods and grunts, the verger recovered himself and said all was okay. Our original agreement would be honoured. It was a huge relief but, to this day I still do not know if Frances's was the first secular funeral ever held in that lovely little church. But I do know one thing: this generosity to unbelievers on the part of the Church of England was an act of what I can only call true Christian charity. It was a kindness for which I will be grateful until my own dying day.

As for the Camino, somehow I felt I had always been aware of it, but it really grabbed my attention in the early 1990s when I read *'Spanish Pilgrimage: A Canter to St James'*, a charming book by the explorer and conservationist Robin Hanbury-Tenison. He and his wife Louella had ridden white Andalusian horses along the *Camino Francés* from Roncesvalles, just on the Spanish side of the Pyrenees, to Santiago. Of Anglo-Irish Protestant descent, Hanbury-Tenison spared his readers much of the religious aspect of the pilgrimage. His was more an ecological embrace of the experience: he used the term 'green pilgrim'. Interestingly, one of his neighbours back home in Cornwall was James Lovelock, originator of the idea of Gaia – the concept of the earth as a self-regulating mechanism.

For my part, the strong points of 'Spanish Pilgrimage' were the historic detail that was skilfully woven into the narrative, the descriptions of the landscape and architecture along the Way and the excellent photographs which whetted my appetite for north west Spain, a region I had not previously considered visiting. In 1994, Frances and I drove down through France and followed the route of the Camino from St Jean Pied de Port, the traditional starting point on the French side of the Pyrenees, to Santiago. With three children in tow – our youngest, Conor, was just five at the time – we were hardly going to walk it. Even if we'd had the inclination, confined to school holidays, we simply didn't have the time.

Though somewhat rushed, the trip had left a kaleidoscope of impressions in my mind. The sad, rundown state of the huge hostelry at Roncesvalles, the pilgrims' first stop after breasting the Pyrenees. The fairytale bishop's palace in Astorga, one of the lesser known works of the remarkable Catalan architect Antoni Gaudi. The raggle taggle of precarious-looking storks' nests on the crockets of the magnificent cathedral at Leon. A blissful, still evening, standing with the children on the elegant 11th century bridge in Puente de la Reina – surely one of the most beautiful of the pilgrim bridges on the Camino – peering down at a long-legged frog swimming lazily through the central arch.

At Frances's insistence, in the parched town of Sahagún, we tracked down the gloomy statue erected to honour a 16th century Benedictine monk, Brother Pedro Ponce de Leon. Working from the simple hand gestures used by monks who were sworn to silence, Brother Pedro developed the first techniques for teaching deaf people how to read, write and speak. Frances, who had herself learned sign language in order to teach deaf students, was keen to pay her respects to this humane pioneer from an age when deaf people were considered simply incapable of being educated.

In 1994, much of the Camino was in a sad state. We saw mere handfuls of pilgrims, many forced to walk for long stretches along the verge of busy main roads. With huge lorries thundering past very close to them, it didn't look like an enjoyable never mind a spiritual experience. And, when we followed tiny country roads to keep close to the trail, they led us through sad, impoverished villages, with few options for accommodation or refreshment.

What we didn't know then was that the Camino was, in fact, in the early stages of its renaissance. Proclaimed in 1987 as the first European Cultural Route by the Council of Europe, the Camino was promoted as a symbol of the connectivity of a shared European culture. More locally, it was utilised as a driving force for the regeneration of the neglected north west of Spain, a region that had suffered more than its share of economic stagnation and population loss. All this focus underpinned and sustained the Way's gradual restoration.

With the dawning of the third millennium, as more and more healthy baby boomers reached retirement age, with the leisure and money to enjoy long hikes, pilgrim numbers began to soar. In 2012 and 2013, when one of my best friends walked the Camino in two tranches, I found myself very envious. But, at that time, Frances was gradually losing the ability to walk independently, so my work as a carer was increasing. A hike of any kind – never mind one as ambitious as a Camino – was out of the question.

All that changed with the unsought freedom of widowerhood. The huge numbers now walking the *Camino Francés*, however, made me consider the less arduous and much less crowded *Portugués* option. And, when my siblings decided to meet up in Porto, it seemed opportune to tack on a walk and finally get my feet pointing towards Santiago.

While the domestic, at times almost obscure, *Camino Portugués* lacked the dramatic, exposed and harsh landscape of parts of the *Francés* – the hot, open plateau of the *Meseta* of Castile and León or the bleak exposed heights where medieval pilgrims banded together for safety in numbers against lurking robbers and worse – I felt its modest demands would better suit my mood and ability. And, as I neared the end of my first year as a widower, the hike could be a way of gently taking leave of Frances – or perhaps of her letting me go and me turning on to the different path my life must now take without her.

In addition – because I could never totally shake off the pernicious Catholicism that had moulded me – there was, inevitably, an element of penance. Not too much, considering some of the upmarket hotels I had booked en route – these hardly represented mortification of the flesh. But there would be enough steep hills and hours of hot, sweaty walking in the summer heat to help me atone for my shortcomings as a husband and carer. For my impatience at times; for the occasions when I hadn't been gentle, loving and physical enough to Frances as her abilities declined. I knew this was part of the ongoing guilt of grief and I was still working it through.

Having mulled all this over, I felt better about the days ahead. I had supplied a purpose for my walk and, perhaps, I might also begin to sketch out a route map to the rest of my life. Full of such thoughts, I strode on over the beautiful ancient bridge that leads to Arcos and, much to my astonishment, shortly after two o'clock, arrived at the Quinta San Miguel, my stopping place for the night. I had walked only about 15 km and, despite the bends and traffic on the N306, felt I had enjoyed a gentle introduction to the Camino.

The Quinta, a collection of rustic baroque buildings behind a high wall, reminded me of similar traditional hotels that Frances and I used to seek out on our road trips through inland Spain. After the heat of the day, all was cool and quiet as I walked into Reception. No one was around but, when a young lad eventually appeared, he seemed greatly amused to find a half-baked, would-be pilgrim ending his walk so pathetically early in the day.

Half-baked pilgrim I may have been but, oh, the joy of shuffling off my rucksack. Nothing could take away from the welcome rush of weightlessness that seemed to lift me from the floor as I laid down my burden. As a neophyte hiker, the feeling was a genuine novelty for me but, over the coming days, at the end of each section of the walk, that sensation of immediate lightness, of a renewed spring in the step from no longer being weighed down by a large sack, was something I never grew tired of.

My 'room' turned out to be a substantial apartment, with its own lobby, complete with couch, table and chairs; a kitchen, equipped not just with kettle, cooker, dishwasher, fridge, sink and microwave, but also stocked with oils and other culinary bits and pieces, as well as a miniature bottle of 10-year-old tawny Port. And then there was the bedroom and bathroom. All were delightfully cool, if rather gloomy. The only natural light came from a small window in the bedroom. With the addition of a minibar, I could avail myself of two fridges to host an impromptu party or simply cool my water bottles (one of which, I was surprised to note, I hadn't even broached on my walk).

Though the walking had been gentle, the day had been hot and was getting still hotter. I was glad to stop and in need of a shower but first, like a true hiker, I had laundry to attend to. I rinsed my shirt, socks and hi-tech underpants in the bathroom basin and draped them on the windowsill. I had been in the Quinta only 15 minutes, but already I was lowering the tone. Fortunately, my apartment was accessed through an archway and separate from the main hotel building, and the window gave on to a secluded area of garden next to the estate wall. So reputational damage to the establishment was kept to a minimum.

To my surprise, I was feeling quite tired so, after my shower, I got into bed and fell asleep. Then, as dinner wasn't due until 8:00 pm, I ate a chorizo and cheese roll I had bought at the airport, with a mug of Earl Grey tea – courtesy of one of the tea bags I had brought with me from England. Rested and refreshed, I set out to see what the sleepy hamlet of Arcos had to offer on a dozy Sunday afternoon.

Not a lot, as it turned out. Immediately next to the Quinta was a fine church, set on a platform accessed by 27 steps – quite a challenge, I would have thought, for aged worshippers on creaky legs. Even more surprisingly, the adjoining cemetery lay up a further flight of steps from the church itself. I am a self-confessed haunter of graveyards – my poor children had been dragged through dozens in their childhood – but I didn't think I'd ever seen one set in a terrace like this, well above its church. Death in Arcos was clearly a step up.

On either side of the church steps two imposing and forbidding bronze busts of clerical eminences sat on stone plinths, their pincer gazes no doubt keeping the faithful in order. One rejoiced in the baleful surname of Salazar. I felt sure his progress through the church hadn't been hindered by blood connection with the dictator's family. His bust certainly captured the face of a self-important, old-school cleric who would have stood no nonsense from the laity.

The only other establishment in the village was a café where I settled in for a couple of beers, the first of which was accompanied by a generous *tapa* of bread, olives and slices of sausage. With dinner still some way off, this was very welcome.

Later, promptly at eight, dressed in my 'formal' off-road evening wear of cotton shirt and shorts, I took my place at the solitary table laid for me in the Quinta's small dining room. No menu was presented as it was a fixed offering for the five of us who were dining. An aged Belgian couple and two women next to me who turned out to be a mother-daughter combination of Brazilian/Danes: the mother was Danish and clearly her daughter's father had been Brazilian. They were fellow Camino walkers who had actually set out from the centre of Porto, so they quickly claimed the moral high ground on me.

The women were pleasant company and we exchanged our wisdom of the Way so far. Having taken hours to reach Arcos, they were determined to set off just after six next morning. I assured them that, if they did, they would be in Barcelos – our target for the next day – for a late lunch.

Dinner consisted of a dull soup followed by an immense plateful of dry veal, rice and beans and chip-like potatoes. All rather mediocre but redeemed by a sturdy Beira Reserva for a reasonable €15. Afterwards I retired to my apartment with a large glass of wine and was pleased to find my washing acceptably dry on its window perch. Hooray for artificial fabric! It had been a manageable first day and, despite twinges of guilt at my underhand starting point, I felt the Camino had baptised and embraced me. I was a *peregrino* of sorts.

Monday 10 July

Arcos to Barcelos

After prolonged discussion with the Quinta's owner about my intention to use an older Camino shortcut out of the village, I set off walking at 9:20. He assured me the shortcut made no difference, whereas the guidebook said it cut 800 metres off the modern route – and, in my view, it had the additional benefit of avoiding a stretch along the main road. After yesterday's zig-zagging on the N306 I was determined to seek out off-road sections wherever I could find them.

So I took the shortcut, which turned out to be a little-used but pleasant, shaded path through dry eucalyptus woods. It delivered me easily to the next small town, Rates, where I dropped into the dignified Romanesque church of São Pedro.

Two churches in two days: what was happening? I was in grave danger of taking pilgrim piety seriously.

When I entered the church, two women, clearly pilgrims, were standing in front of the altar. As they turned to leave through a side door, we greeted one another and moments later one came back in to speak to me. She apologised for interrupting my prayers but I assured her it wasn't necessary: I hadn't been praying. She wanted to know how they could get their *Credencial* stamped, there being no sign of clergy or anyone else in the church.

The women turned out to be Canadians who had just started their Camino after taking a taxi from their hotel in Porto to Rates. Style points indeed! I gave them the benefit of the vast knowledge I had gleaned over the previous day, particularly about the ability to get a *credencial* stamp in pretty well any local shop, hotel or bar. And I explained how advisable it was to take deviations when offered, even if it meant adding a kilometre or two to the journey. Then I left them to orientate themselves and wandered off at my own pace, leaving the sleepy village behind.

The day was hot and the route became quite hilly, so the next few kilometres put my lightweight, wicking sports gear to the test. I was glad to stop for lunch at café restaurant Pedra Ferada, where, on entering, I was greeted by the Brazilian/

Danish mother and daughter. They were just beginning their first course and, when they learned that I had set off at 9:20, they were shocked that I had caught up with them so quickly. They had started walking shortly after eight, so clearly their planned 6:00 am reveille had proved overambitious.

They invited me to join them and, when I shuffled off my rucksack, their faces fell a little further with the realisation that I was carrying a full pack. Their luggage was being shipped on to their next destination – a common practice on the Camino, leaving walkers to carry just a day sack. Their target for the following day was Ponte de Lima – a daunting 35 kilometres – and they were clearly dreading it. I didn't help much when, a trifle smugly perhaps, I said I had decided to split that section with an overnight stop half-way.

The pilgrim's menu provided a sound and comforting bowl of cabbage and bean soup with a main course of veal (again), rice, potatoes and salad. The meat was much better than the previous evening's offering at the Quinta but, when I requested hot sauce such as Peri Peri to perk up the rice, I got into trouble.

In no uncertain terms, the *maitre d'* explained that the meal had to be sampled first before any adulteration could be considered. And, clearly, in his view, sauce was not the thing with this particular dish. But eventually he relented and provided a grainy bowl of pleasingly fiery stock that helped soften everything up.

Just then the two Canadian women entered, so there were greetings and introductions all round. They, too, were carrying day packs and were very pleased with their morning's progress. The Danes left and, at their invitation, I swopped to the Canadians' table. One was wearing an unmissable maple leaf T-shirt, so we discussed how Canadians abroad always need to make it absolutely clear they're not Americans – particularly in the current times. We agreed that, in the wider world, it's better to be Canadian than American, in the same way that it's better to be Irish than English! On that note of concord I took my leave. My bill for the pilgrim's menu, a large beer and a coffee came to a very acceptable €7.50.

Uphill from the café I crossed a busy road to take an optional – but, in my view, now obligatory – deviation through a forested hillside. This turned out to be exactly what the guidebook had promised: 'a strenuous uphill climb', but, as much of it was through shady woodland, it was well worth the effort.

Eventually the path dropped down and I tried to find my way into the centre of Barcelos, one of the larger towns on the route. I went wrong at one point but, seeing my mistake, the driver of a white van reversed towards me and kindly set me in the right direction. Reaching the impressive riverfront, I crossed the fine bridge that leads to the historic centre. Barcelos is a beautifully presented town, with a well-preserved commercial heart and a huge plaza that hosts one of the largest and liveliest markets in Portugal every Thursday.

The symbol of Barcelos – a multicoloured rooster with a flame-red, upright cockscomb on top of his perky head – is ubiquitous throughout the town. It is found in the form of ceramic figures, fridge magnets, posters, T-shirts – even toothpick holders – and has become an unofficial symbol for Portugal itself. It is also used as the logo for the restaurant chain Nando's, purveyors of tongue-tingling peri peri chicken to the masses.

The story behind the rooster mirrors an identical legend attached to the ancient town of Santo Domingo de Calzada, an important stop on the Rioja section of the *Camino Francés*. In Santo Domingo, however, rather than ceramic versions, a live cockerel and chicken are kept in a glass-fronted henhouse, mounted high inside the cathedral, where they are a major tourist attraction. The crowing of a cockerel in such an unlikely setting certainly delighted our children and Frances and me, too, when we visited in 1994.

The legend in both towns is very similar and concerns an unfortunate pilgrim who was sentenced to hang for theft, despite protesting his innocence to the judge who condemned him. Before being taken to the gallows, he tells the judge that the roast cockerel gracing the judicial dining table would come to life as proof of his guiltlessness. Despite this, the poor lad is hanged but, that evening, when the salivating judge finally sits down to dinner, the crisply cooked fowl on his plate leaps up and crows. Horrified, the judge rushes to the gallows to find the condemned man still alive – saved by the miracle of the resurgent cock.

I do not know why two such separate towns should have identified themselves with the same myth but – a resurrected rooster – what a brilliant piece of marketing for a medieval pilgrimage! Even in our Viagra-saturated days, perhaps, the prospect of a revitalised cock could still put a spring in the step of many an ageing pilgrim.

I wandered the town for a bit, then found a bar in the huge market plaza where I settled in the shade with a beer while I phoned my friend Andrew Jahoda, who happened to be holidaying nearby with his family. We had arranged that I would spend the night with them and I was looking forward to catching up on all that had happened since I had last seen them in Glasgow some years previously.

Andrew picked me up in his hire car and we headed for their holiday villa on a country estate in the hills above

Barcelos. A very enjoyable evening ensued. Andrew's barbecued sardines were fresher and sweeter than those we had eaten in Porto. His brother Colin contributed a calamari and vegetable fry, while Andrew's partner Lorna produced succulent chicken pieces which were finished off on the barbecue.

It was a typically raucous, indulgent and extended Jahoda family supper, a heart-warming coda to an easy second day on the pilgrim trail.

Tuesday 11 July

Barcelos to Seara

Following an indulgent and prolonged *al fresco* breakfast, Andrew dropped me around 10:30 on the north side of Barcelos, near the football stadium. This was another slight cheat on my part but it saved walking out from the town centre past the ring road and through the dreary suburbs. Ring roads and suburbs formed no part of my Camino plans.

I was soon in the countryside and quickly caught up with my Canadian companions from the previous day. Like me, they had made a late start and were now indulging in a rest stop, so I left them to it and walked on through pleasant country lanes that led to a steep climb up to Tamel San Pedro Fins, just below our high point for the day. The temperature was much hotter than Monday and I hugged any shade I could find.

After the sweat of the climb, an easy, country section delivered me to a modern, clean café for lunch. Once he had set me up with beer and water, the owner explained that the dish of the day was scallops and pork. At the mention of scallops I became very excited but thought them a strange combination with pork. When the dish eventually arrived, it turned out to be escalopes of pork with, of course, not a scallop in sight. This time, however, the patron was happy to respond to my request for Peri Peri sauce. Clearly, word had got out that a mad Irish chilli nut was loose on the Camino.

At nearly 35 kilometres, the stage from Barcelos to Ponte de Lima is the longest on the *Camino Portugués*, but I was under no pressure as I had selected a handy stopover for the night at about the 20-kilometre mark. The yellow arrow waymarks, which are a useful feature of the Camino, were sometimes confusing and certainly much less frequent than on previous days. Perhaps the local Camino confraternity was not quite as active as their brethren in the immediate vicinity of Barcelos.

The afternoon's walk saw stretches of sandy track alternating with harder cobblestone sections. It had a timeless, ancient feel and I settled into an easy, relaxed rhythm.

It may have been due to the hazy heat, but occasionally I had a feeling of being in no man's land, in both time and space. All was utterly peaceful and beautiful: everything I had hoped the Camino would be. There were many lovely spots and plenty of shade. At one point, I found myself crossing a low-slung, medieval bridge, the Ponte das Tábuas, where an old man patiently dangled a fishing line into the river, with no obvious expectation of success.

As I had been unsure, before setting out, what my daily mileage capacity might be, I had booked accommodation only for the beginning and end of my hike and for my two-night stopover in Tui for the mid-Camino weekend. I was happy to leave the other nights to chance and hoped to find a bed wherever I fetched up at the end of a day's walking.

My target lodgings for that night were a converted stable block at Casa de Valhinos which I was confident of striking. But, despite following the Camino arrows assiduously, I somehow missed it. For a while I wasn't exactly sure where I was, but, even though it meant having to walk much further than my previously intended stopping point, I resolved to carry on rather than turn back.

The afternoon grew oppressively hot and I was beginning to tire. One blistered foot was painful and my arthritic left knee started to complain. I swallowed a sadly melted Mars bar I had carried since Porto and considered my options. The map promised three Quinta (country estate) hotels and a pilgrim house which offered beds for the night, so I limped gamely on. One of these would surely accommodate me.

When I reached it, the first Quinta presented imposing but firmly locked doors. There was no response when I tolled the rope attached to the large, sonorous bell hanging above the entrance and phone calls to the number in the guidebook also yielded nothing. Some workmen, who were placing granite setts in a driveway opposite, informed me the place was closed and the same held true for the next mute and bolted Quinta. As for the Camino *casa*, a spacious modern house, it appeared to be totally deserted.

Hot, sticky and sore of foot, I soldiered on and eventually arrived at an impressive, pillared gateway that guarded the entrance to the third and final Quinta. All my hopes were now pinned on this. I trudged the length of the driveway, through extensive grounds, to reach an attractive but seemingly deserted establishment. The door was open so I mooched around through various empty rooms until I finally ran to earth a woman working in the kitchen. Adopting my neediest pilgrim pose – not too difficult as I was already a sorry, dust-encrusted sight, I asked if I could have a room for the night. Making it clear the decision did not lie with her and that she would have to phone someone, my potential saviour dived into the depths of the building. She returned suspiciously swiftly, shook her head sadly and muttered a firm but crushing *'Non'*.

Distinctly unimpressed by this unchristian attitude to a forlorn *peregrino*, I summoned up what dignity I could muster and trudged back down the long drive to resume the Way. At this point I was only about eight kilometres from Ponte de Lima, my destination for the following night, but I knew I wouldn't make it. My left foot was too sore, my arthritic knee ached and I badly needed beer and dinner (in that order!).

Despite my discomfort I was far from despairing. Hunting for *ad hoc* lodgings was something I'd become familiar with during many forays with Frances. In August 1976 we flew to Venice for the first time on a busy Friday evening. Our flight being delayed didn't help our last-minute search for a hotel room at the height of the tourist season. Undaunted, we wandered from St Mark's Square towards the Rialto, inquiring hopefully at every hotel we passed. The response was the same everywhere: *'Completo. Completo'*.

Then, in the San Leo, an eccentric establishment about half-way between those two tourist honeypots, our plight drew some sympathy from the harassed proprietor. Like the others, he explained, his hotel was full. No one would have a room free on a Friday night, but the next day was Saturday – changeover day – when space would certainly be freed up. But, he said, as he and his wife had plans to stay up all night playing cards with friends, we might as well have their bedroom. In a state of some astonishment, we were shown into the impressive marital boudoir where we happily passed our first night in Venice, cocooned in a huge, elaborately sculpted Italian bed, under the guilt-inducing shadow of a massive crucifix.

Two years before our Venetian holiday, during an epic road trip through 22 of the continental United States, we found ourselves heading west through the Arizona desert as night fell. The fuel gauge on the monstrously thirsty, gold and cream Lincoln Continental Mark IV that we were delivering from New York to Hollywood had dropped ominously into the red. We were travelling through a Navajo reservation and, while campfires flickered far off on either side of the empty two-lane highway, no towns or villages could be seen. Fortunately, the map promised a place called Teec Nos Pos a little way down the line, so gingerly I nursed the car onward.

Suddenly, in the darkness of the desert night, the comforting strip lights of a petrol station came into view. As we pulled off the road to fill up, it became clear this was a gathering place for local Navajo youths. One of them sauntered lazily over to the car and began pouring fuel into our echoingly empty tank.

While he did so. I quizzed him about the possibility of finding a hotel or motel nearby. He explained there was a hotel some 30 or 40 miles in one direction and a motel a similar distance along the road we were following.

'What about this place called Teec Nos Pos?' I asked.

Without batting an eyelid he replied: 'You're downtown.'

Flushed with the contentment that only a full tank of petrol can bring, we travelled on until a low, barely lit building, squatting all by itself on the roadside, persuaded us this was our magnificent motel for the night. By then it was probably nearly one in the morning and there was no sign of life about the place. I found a bell and pressed on it insistently for what seemed like ten minutes.

My efforts were rewarded when lights came on and an outbreak of coughing and cursing from the interior preceded the arrival of a slippered and dressing gown-clad figure who, not surprisingly, was far from overjoyed to see us. It felt like a Hitchcockian scene but, I was relieved to note, this was definitely mother Norma, not Norman, who rasped a grumpy greeting.

The 'Psycho' comparisons ended swiftly, however, as we were shown into a spacious, wood-lined room open to the desert sky through a large hole in the ceiling. Like the opening above the atrium in a Roman villa, this was air conditioning of the most basic kind in the Arizona desert. And it was staggeringly effective – it was one of the coldest places we had ever slept in but, as we shivered, we were amply compensated by the sight of the desert stars twinkling above our heads.

Even after our children came along, Frances and I continued to take a *laissez faire* approach to en route accommodation as we travelled each summer through France, Italy or Spain. Many and frequent were the howls from the three little people in the back seat as I climbed back into the car, having been rebuffed by another hotel or roadhouse which had no need of our custom that night. Feeling the pressure on one occasion I growled: 'Well, now you know how Mary and Joseph felt that first Christmas Eve in Bethlehem. Perhaps there'll be a farmer up the road who'll let us use his stable.' Needless to say, the back seat howls merely doubled in volume.

But somehow it always worked out. We never had to resort to sleeping in the car – never mind a stable. – though once we were forced, reluctantly, to descend well after midnight from the hills of Tuscany and pay through the nose for rooms in a nondescript business hotel in an anonymous and hideous town.

Based on past form therefore, I remained confident I would still find somewhere to lay my pilgrim head and squeeze my penitential blisters. Squinting again at the guidebook map,

I noticed a hotel marked on the main road, about 400 metres west of the Camino. I struggled on but, when I reached the road and turned off the Way, I could see no sign of a hotel. Reluctantly I turned back towards Ponte de Lima, determined at least to find a beer and a place to rest my hot and bothered feet. I was just about to rejoin the Camino when an old Mercedes, parked right where the path issued out on to the main road, caught my eye. Through his wing mirror, the driver was, I felt, watching me closely.

As I drew level, he asked if I was looking for the hotel. I said I had been but couldn't find it. He assured me it was nearby and offered to drive me there. Before the words had quite left his mouth I was in his passenger seat. We drove just past the bend where I had turned back and there it was, with flags flying: the Residêncial Pinheiro Manso. It may have been a modern roadhouse but it was a very welcome sight.

The driver turned out to be the owner and the Residêncial was very much a family affair. His wife, son and French daughter-in-law worked alongside him, helping run the place. Perhaps the owner was in the habit of loitering at the point where the Camino spilled out on to the main road in the hope of drumming up trade. The Residêncial could certainly do with it. Despite its fluttering flags and prominent location on the main road to Ponte de Lima, there appeared to be no other guests. And I soon learned that, not only was its position wrongly marked on my map, its status as a Residéncial – a lower category than a hotel – meant it had no restaurant. But, once we settled on French as our common language, the friendly receptionist/daughter-in-law assured me they could rustle up a pizza and salad for my dinner.

Grabbing three cold beers and a bottle of water, I ordered my banquet for 7:30 and set off up the stairs to my room which, fortunately, turned out to be on the first floor. A great consolation after 27 hot and sticky kilometres.

Like the hardened Caminista I felt I had now become, my first task was to rinse out my walking gear and hang it on the balcony rails. More flags for the Residéncial and a nice touch, I thought, for passing traffic, though my sodden smalls would probably repel rather than entice further guests.

Taking off my shoes, I noticed melted tar stuck between the grooves of the soles. Tarry roads had been few and far between that day but the rural ones were melting and sticky in the heat. I examined my left foot and regretted not packing a sewing kit. I would have liked to have burst the blister before dressing it with Compeed, those blessed padded plasters that are every hiker's friend.

After a shower and having consumed all three beers, I headed down to dinner. I ordered a gin and tonic as an aperitif but a salad was swiftly produced instead. Alas, this consisted of about 60 per cent cucumber – a vegetable I cannot abide – with a further 20 per cent made up of green tomatoes. I later learned the Portuguese are very fond of their green tomatoes and very good they are too, but, in my ignorance on first acquaintance, I treated them with disdain as simply unripe.

The promised pizza followed rapidly, accompanied by a glass of wine – by this point I'd given up on the G&T. The pizza was a stodgy example of the breed that shared absolutely no DNA with Naples' finest. True to form, I requested chilli sauce or Peri Peri. This caused the usual consternation and the receptionist was summoned to check what I'd actually asked for. She gamely produced a puddle of oil in a little dish but warned me I should *'faites attention'*. I was expecting a fiery kick but, instead, it had a cloying undertone that I thought I remembered from childhood as the taste of castor oil. Clearly there was no way this pizza was going to be improved. Rather ungratefully, I scraped off the toppings, ate them and left the rest.

Finally, my gin and tonic arrived, complete with strawberries for some reason. Opting to treat this as both pudding and *digestif*, I moved to the garden at the back of the hotel where I sat by the empty swimming pool in the fading sunlight. As I sipped what was the most flavoursome thing I had held to my lips that evening, I realised I would never have a gin in Spain or Portugal without thinking of Frances and the delight she took in the huge glass chalices in which her favourite tipple was invariably served in Iberia.

Just before midnight I settled down to sleep. Having covered 27 kilometres, I was left with only about seven to reach Ponte de Lima next day. I could look forward to a restful afternoon, wandering round the town before hooking up again in the evening with the Jahoda family who were coming to Ponte de Lima to join me for dinner.

I just hoped they weren't thinking of ordering pizza.

Wednesday 12 July

Seara to Ponte de Lima

Fortified by a breakfast of ham, cheese, bread rolls, orange squash and coffee, I paid my bill and bade farewell to my kindly Residéncial rescuers. The total came to €53 (€35 for bed and breakfast and €18 for three beers, a large bottle of water, gin and tonic, glass of wine and dinner!) – truly astonishing value.

I set off just after ten and an easy 6.5 kilometres took me through sleepy hamlets and under shady vine-covered pergolas to the fine riverside at Ponte de Lima. Nearing the town I greeted a fellow pilgrim, a woman resting on a stone bench beside the water. There was no response. This was unusual on the Camino where a cheery bonhomie normally subsists among hikers, but perhaps she had caught a whiff of my lack of piety or, more likely, my suppurating feet. Further along, another female hiker had stopped to photograph the elegant bridge that spans the impressively broad river Lima. A large 'Ireland' tricolour patch was sewn to the back of her rucksack, so I inquired if she was indeed Irish. Without a word, she wheeled round from the river, camera in hand, and took my photograph.

This was my strange and slightly unnerving introduction to Simone, who turned out not to be Irish, but German – from near Hamburg. But she loved Ireland – like, she said, most of her fellow countrymen. I suspected that flaunting an Irish flag on her bag might make for more friendly openings in some places than a Deutschland badge. With our long history of not invading anyone, we Irish like to think we are welcome everywhere – at least nowadays. It wasn't always so.

Simone was another Camino veteran. She had already walked the *Francés* and was an enthusiast for the delights of pilgrim hostels: 'They're cheap and you meet interesting people from all over the world,' she assured me, urging me to give them a try. I said I might at some point but, truth be told, I had no intention of doing so. During five miserable years at boarding school I had had more than my fill of dormitories. I had no wish to revisit the experience. And now, as a man in his mid-sixties who appreciated his comforts, I was happy to stick to hotels. Frankly, as the previous day had confirmed, at the end of a sweaty mid-summer hike, my needs were more readily met by an en suite and a mini bar.

In search of such consolation, I made the Tourist Information office my first stop in Ponte de Lima where I asked for the best hotel in town. A helpful lady recommended the Imperio do Norte, an austere-looking, modern block which stood right on the riverfront with a profusion of magnificent mature plane trees immediately in front.

Assessing my dusty shoes and rucksack down the length of her haughty nose, the receptionist clearly doubted my suitability for her recently refurbished establishment. She confirmed there was availability but 'perhaps I should tell you how much it costs first?' Undaunted, I paid a far from extortionate €50 upfront to secure a corner riverside room with balcony.

After the obligatory laundry session, I set out to find some lunch and see the town. The day was getting very hot, so I settled with a beer on the terrace of a restaurant with ample shade and a good view of the bridge and river. Though it was somewhat touristy, I decided this was as good a place as any to eat and so ordered vegetarian tagliatelle and Padrón peppers. A kind waitress anointed the pasta with the last precious drops from a venerable bottle of Tabasco. This was just as well as, despite there being a generous plateful of about three dozen peppers, not one delivered the slightest tingle of heat.

True or not, I've always understood that about one in ten Padrón peppers is supposed to be hot – though this may well be just a clever promotional myth. People who fear chillies feel safe eating them, on the basis that the odds are in their favour, while people like me – who relish a mouth-blistering hurtle along the Scoville scale – devour them in hope of striking a fiery exception. No luck so far.

After lunch I wandered about the old town and then crossed the elegant stone bridge, on which a dramatic sculpture of a wild-haired pilgrim wished *'Bom Caminho'* to passing hikers. Street sculptures of rural scenes, including a jolly peasant wedding party, lined the riverbank where a column of cut-out models of Roman soldiers marched determinedly towards the water. This, it transpired, marked the spot where legionaries had waded across in the days of the empire.

Ponte de Lima was busy with visitors. It claims to be the oldest town in Portugal and is a popular tourist destination as well as a Camino hub. During lunch I found myself surrounded by a jolly gang of pensioners, all wearing identical distinctive hats and clearly part of an organised coach trip. Pilgrims of all shapes and sizes wandered about – many of whom I doubted would ever make the distance.

After lunch, from the bridge, I watched a group of kayakers under instruction in mid-river. Despite a lifelong antipathy to water-based activities that don't involve a boat with a fridge, I have always thought kayaking an elegant and graceful sport. Perhaps Ponte de Lima was the place to learn.

Back across the river and safely in the shade of another riverside café, I noticed a hefty female pilgrim wander past, flanked by two male companions. None of them noticed when a sandal dropped from the side of her rucksack and, when I called after them, they didn't respond. Leaving my coffee, I picked up the sandal and managed to catch them just as they turned onto the bridge. As I restored her sandal to her, I received fulsome thanks from the portly lady who was already sweating profusely. It was my modest good deed for the day but I couldn't help thinking the three of them had a tough few hours ahead of them.

By this time the heat had become extreme – the hottest day yet, I was sure. This filled me with some trepidation for the steep ascent the guidebook promised for the following day. My knee was still rather painful. I just hoped it wasn't going to prove problematic on the climb.

I returned to my hotel to get ready for the evening. On the terrace bar I medicated myself with the usual large G&T, thinking, of course, of Frances. G&Ts in Portugal may be as generously proportioned as those in Spain but they are undeniably weaker. Thus, only modestly fortified, I met up with my friends who, unlike me, had spent an active afternoon diving into chilly waterfall pools in the rugged and unfrequented hills of the Ponte de Lima hinterland.

After a seafood dinner of trencherman proportions, we joined the audience at a free outdoor jazz concert, part of a series of music events the town hosted in July. A duo called Songbird – a subtle pianist and the most astonishingly skilled double bass player I had ever heard – treated us to a string of cool, mellifluous classics and newer numbers unknown to me. It was a bonus ending to an indulgent and restful day.

After bidding farewell to my friends, I walked back along the quiet riverfront in the warm, balmy night. Ponte de Lima had rested me well and shown itself to be a delightful, beautifully situated town. It was a place to which I might well one day return.

Thursday 13 July

Ponte de Lima to Casa de Capela

Banal piped music playing in the dining room didn't help my mood at breakfast. With the prospect of 'the steepest accumulative climb' of the *Camino Portugués* ahead of me, I was somewhat apprehensive. And, for once, Mr Brierley didn't offer much reassurance: the contour cross-section in his guidebook certainly made the ascent look dramatic. Resigned to my fate, I set off at 8:15, crossing Ponte de Lima's beautiful arched bridge for the final time and muttering farewell to the Christ-like carving wishing me *'Bom Caminho'*.

The walking was pleasant – even a section under what I assumed was motorway – and got better as the day progressed. I encountered a number of pilgrims but we didn't fall in together, just wished one another *'Buen Camino'* and carried on our way. At the last café before the main ascent, a group of five hikers were stretched out, happily relaxed and showing no signs of urgency to tackle the impending climb.

The day was beginning to get very hot and, when I realised I was carrying only a litre of water, I stopped at a trout fishery to pick up 2.5 litres – more than I had carried on any previous day. But, as no water would be available between the *Fonte Três Bicas*, a triple channel spring at the start of the main ascent, and the summit of the climb, it seemed a sensible precaution.

Up to this point the walk had been a gentle, birdsong-filled ramble along verdant pathways – what we would call green lanes in England – and totally delightful. But gradually the ascent got steeper and more rock-strewn. I pressed on, stopping frequently to drink. Beads of my sweat dusted the Camino like diamonds glinting in the sun. I was keen to get to the top before the full heat of the day kicked in. For a time, I followed in the footsteps of an agile young couple who were walking very easily, with light packs and carrying no water, as far as I could see.

The climb was relentless: it was a case of just trudging stolidly on. Sometimes we seemed to be clambering up through a steep rocky gorge of what could have been a dried up riverbed. But I felt it was manageable and, while I couldn't say I was enjoying myself, I was happy to deal with whatever presented itself. Nearing the top, I placed a rock for Frances at the foot of a stone cross, the aptly named *Cruz dos Franceses*. According to John Brierley, this cross, also referred to as the *Cruz dos Mortos*, commemorates an ambush of Napoleonic troops during the Peninsular War. What the poor buggers were doing up there was anyone's guess.

Suddenly, I noticed the trees were all hung with untidy plastic bags that seemed to contain old tissues or wads of cotton wool. The contents had turned to a murky liquid mess and it was all very unsightly. Showing my naive urban instincts, my first thought was that perhaps the bags had been put there to encourage hikers to deposit their used tissues in them rather than litter the forest floor. But, when I saw that trees set back from the path also had bags attached, I realised this was actually a far from picturesque method of tapping for pine resin. It was clearly an extensive enterprise, but it must have been a marathon task to collect the produce. Perhaps the harvesters used mules to reach the more remote parts of the forest. It was certainly a laborious way to scent one's disinfectant.

Finally, emerging from the woods just below the summit, I added another stone for Frances to a ramshackle cairn. Four people, who had passed me earlier when I stopped to gulp some water on the way up, had assembled here. Two were the couple I had followed earlier and the young woman greeted me warmly. This made me regret not picking up a pink baseball cap I'd noticed on the ground a while back and which I thought might have been hers. Of course I couldn't have counted on seeing her again, but clearly – despite the sandal restitution of yesterday – my adherence to pilgrim kindness still had some way to go.

The others were a much older couple. I noticed the woman, sporting a prominent cross hanging from her neck, when she and her companion walked past me earlier. She had greeted me in a friendly fashion but he totally ignored me – as he had done outside the café where they were among the group of hikers resting before the ascent.

They were now seated on the only bench close to the summit. It was happily in the shade and they had plonked their rucksacks on the seat alongside them, taking up the entire space.

I made a move towards the bench, not actually intending to sit there but interested to see how they would react. They were both muttering prayers: he was calling out from a little black book and she was responding. It was exactly noon so they were perhaps reciting the Angelus. At any rate, they made no attempt to shift their rucksacks. Clearly they were too absorbed in higher things to make room for some lesser soul to relax alongside them. What a fine example of public piety in action, I thought, as I left them to it.

Having conquered the climb – which had been tough in the heat but hadn't quite justified the grim forebodings in the guidebook, I was keen to celebrate with an appropriate chilled liquid. Signs promised the delights of the Roulote Bar a couple of kilometres downhill so, despite both knees complaining vociferously, I pressed on.

As I swung into the courtyard of the bar I was greeted by Simone, the German woman I had encountered on the way into Ponte de Lima. She said she had just been talking about me. She was lunching with an American from Washington DC and two Catalans – definitely *not* Spaniards, as one of them quickly made clear – called Pep and Jefe.

I joined them and ordered a large beer. When only a small bottle arrived, I protested that our host clearly hadn't understood that his clientele now included a thirsty Irishman. On the Camino, I knew, national stereotypes had to be adhered to at all costs.

Much multinational badinage ensued while I tucked into flame-cooked chicken and salad. Jefe, a rotund Falstaffian character, held court – in Spanish rather than Catalan as a gesture towards the rest of us. He barely let anyone else get a word in. Luckily I was occupied with eating. I don't usually appreciate my own loquaciousness being circumscribed, but Jefe was clearly determined to live up to his name as 'chief' among men.

The quiet American quickly departed and was replaced by a striking young woman from the Savoy region of France. I had encountered her earlier, resting in a shady spot on one of the steeper rock wall ascents. She was wearing an exceptionally large and, to my mind, very heavy straw sombrero. Jefe immediately decided that, from her dark looks, she must have some Mexican in her to match her choice of headgear.

Barely pausing for breath, Jefe continued to hold forth, making little allowance for those of us who couldn't keep up with his cascade of Castilian. He was a proud heavy metal fan and rather puzzled by our failure to share his fervour for Metallica, Deep Purple and their ilk. He resorted to showing videos on his phone of bands torturing their instruments at the many gigs and festivals he had attended. This drew an eager response from Simone, who promptly dug into her own musical archives to play tracks of similar charm. Phones were passed to and fro amid much singing and swaying.

Despite my failure to add to the heavy metal chorus, I got the feeling that Jefe had somehow decided I should be his new best friend on the Camino and he was very keen that we should arrange to meet up along the route. Now, while Jefe was fine company for lunch, I certainly didn't want to spend the afternoon walking with him. I feared it might be a reprise of the voluble Frenchman from the first day, with no easy means of escape.

I explained I was pressing on and also stopping for two nights in Tui, whereas they were walking every day without a break. Eventually, Jefe said how much he had enjoyed our conversation. Rather ungraciously, but to Simone's great amusement, I replied that it hadn't been so much a conversation as a monologue.

When Simone, the French woman and the Catalans began making preparations to move on together, I determined to get ahead of them. I valued the peaceful solitude of my walk too much to become subsumed even on the periphery of a gang. Quickly shouldering my bag, I said my brief goodbyes and exploded out of the gate. Hat on, head down, I scorched off down the hill, walking poles sparking on the road.

I was following the yellow Camino arrows but, in my haste to get away, clearly missed a turn-off on to a rustic lane. After a time I realised I must have gone wrong. I was no longer encountering Camino signs and I really wasn't sure where I was on the map. I reached a crossroads which I hoped might orientate me but, instead of checking the signs and road numbers myself, I went into a shop to ask for directions. The shopkeeper was busy with a customer who wished to post a large parcel. This involved much weighing, measuring and debate about the options. Eventually, a tiny old lady who, like me, was waiting resignedly for attention, assured me the Camino lay straight ahead.

I set off down the road but, after a bit, looking at the road number and checking the map, I decided I was definitely on the wrong track. I flagged down a passing car and the helpful driver, speaking impeccable English, explained where the Camino ran: straight ahead from the shop, for sure, but at right angles to where I had carried on. He offered to drive me there and I gladly accepted, still hoping to keep ahead of Simone, Sombrero and the Catalan brigade.

Opening the rear door, I was about to fling in my rucksack when I noticed a small child cowering on the back seat. Suitably shocked, I held on to the bag and squeezed into the front beside the driver. It would indeed have been poor recompense for his kindness had I crushed his child under ten kilos of rucksack.

Back on the right road, which the Camino followed for a short stretch, I saw all four of my lunch companions – Simone in her straw hat, Jefe and Pep and the Savoyarde in her sombrero. Spotting them at the same time, my driver clearly thought he should drop off this lost soul with these obviously more assured Caministas. But, as I now knew where I was, I objected strongly and urged him to carry on for a few more metres to the point where the Camino parted company with the road.

As we passed the merry quartet – Jefe still gesticulating and talking – I crouched down in my seat, desperate not to be seen. Luckily, they were all either enraptured or browbeaten by the latest tales of Catalan capers, so we passed unnoticed. The Camino lay round a bend, and, in a repeat of my original performance on the outskirts Porto, I quickly hopped out, thanked the driver and stepped away from the road before shouldering my rucksack. Somewhat chastened, I resumed my walk, feeling that, while I may have kept my lead, I had, once again, forfeited any moral advantage.

The track eventually switched back across the road into another idyllic stretch alongside a series of rushing waterfalls. A sign near an ancient bridge informed me I was following Roman road XIX, an important route for the empire, which originally ran from Braga in Portugal to Astorga in northwest Spain. After the morning's climb, all was utterly beautiful and gentle, though the heat was, if anything, more fierce than at midday. In the warm haze of such timeless surroundings I would not have been surprised had a ghostly squad of legionaries materialised alongside me.

Finally, after a long rising section, I came to what I hoped would be my destination for the night – the Casa da Capela, a quiet, unpretentious Quinta where I secured a room for €60. Again, there was no restaurant but, much more importantly at this point, there was an honesty bar and plenty of cold beer in the fridge. After the receptionist had supplied me with two bottles of Sagres and a glass of iced water, freely available from the American-style fridge, I adjourned to my room.

I sat on the bed and removed every item of sodden clothing. It had been an exceptionally hot day. The climb had been tough but, if that was the worst the Camino could throw at me, I had nothing to fear.

In the absence of dining facilities I was told we would be taken by car to a nearby restaurant and delivered back by the restaurant staff. The only other guest they were expecting was a cyclist who eventually arrived, hot and sweaty, after having – to my astonishment – ridden up the rock face on a hired mountain bike.

David was a likeable Colombian, who was currently living in Madrid. He talked about the situation in his home country and his worries for his young family who were still there. He was, unsurprisingly, desperate for them to join him in Spain. Together we travelled to the restaurant in a Mercedes driven by our receptionist. It was clear we were not the only ones heading there for dinner: lots of other Caministas were being dropped off from various lodgings in the vicinity. It must have been the only restaurant for miles.

The first people I saw were Laurie and Carolyn, the two Canadian hikers I had last seen at their rest stop outside Barcelos. David and I joined them and I ordered hake and chips from the Pilgrims' menu.

At some point during the meal Laurie asked me why I was doing the Camino. I explained that, having first thought it was just for the history and the experience of the walk, I had quickly realised that I was actually doing it as a way of saying goodbye to Frances.

Laurie replied that she had heard it said that, if someone didn't know why they were doing the walk, the Camino would reveal it to them along the way. After my experience on the first day, with memories of Frances stirring through my head, I couldn't disagree. Meanwhile, Carolyn and David were both shedding sympathetic tears for my loss.

Despite the sadness of some of our conversation, we had a jolly evening and a group photo was taken – my first with other people on the Camino. As the Canadians were leaving, Carolyn invited me to join them for dinner at the Pousada in Valença the following night. I readily accepted and very much looked forward to seeing them again.

Friday 14 July

Casa da Capela to Tui

Despite the exertions of the previous day's climb, I slept badly. At least two intimidating mosquitoes had invaded my room and I can never sleep with the zizzz of the little bastards sounding in my ears. I killed one and may have accounted for another but couldn't in all conscience claim it, so failed to relax. The insect invasion was my own fault because, in search of cool air, I had left both bedroom and bathroom windows open – a silly thing to do, as the receptionist gleefully assured me in the morning.

I breakfasted with David, who was aiming to complete his cycling Camino from Porto to Santiago in just a week. After yesterday's slow progress, he was keen to clock up some rapid kilometres. The rules for acquiring a *Compostela* require hikers to walk the final 100 km but cyclists have to do 200 km. By this point, after four days on the road, my *Credencial* was beginning to look quite respectable. After obtaining the Casa da Capela's gratifyingly picturesque stamp, I was ready to resume the Way. My feet and legs were sore from the previous day's climb but I had only about 16 kilometres to walk to reach the Parador at Tui and then I would be taking a day off.

I set off shortly after nine, up the hill to the highest point of the day. It felt good to get that over with while the air was relatively cool. The walk provided a mix of shady lanes, back roads and one horrible section along a main road where I felt I must have gone wrong again. But no, eventually the yellow arrows resumed so I was definitely on the Camino.

As I passed a small shrine built into the garden wall of a village house, choral music suddenly struck up. It was triggered, I presumed, by a movement sensor, but surely it must drive the locals mad if every passing dog or cat could set a tinny 'Ave Maria' ringing out through the streets?

This was just another of the surreal moments that the Camino would occasionally toss one's way. Heading into Ponte de Lima on Wednesday morning, a slight movement on my left caught my eye. I turned to see the majestic sight of a large, blow-up plastic flamingo, in a particularly garish pink, moving serenely along the surface of an unseen swimming pool. Amusing and wonderfully weird.

Then there was the elegant Japanese lady who floated towards me, utterly alone, on a rough country lane outside Barcelos. In full Madame Butterfly kimono, holding up a delicate parasol and carrying nothing else, she sailed silently past me with tiny, gliding footsteps – a dignified, serene and composed figure. Off she drifted, heading away from Santiago towards Fatima perhaps – a totally surreal vision.

At one point in the 'spiritual' musings that pepper his guidebook, John Brierley mentions a young Japanese woman who walked from France to Santiago and then just kept going. Perhaps my Camino kimono-wearer was this same woman some years down the line.

Still keeping to my resolution of the first day, on the outskirts of Valença, the last outpost in Portugal before the Camino crossed the river into Spain, I took a slightly longer deviation to avoid having to use the road on the way into town. Then, walking up the hill towards the centre, I was hailed from a bar across the street. There was Simone, with Jefe, Pep and a couple of Spanish girls from Valencia. I joined them for a beer – my second of the day (it was only twelve o'clock!) – but Jefe and I didn't engage this time. Perhaps my monologue remark of the previous day had festered.

Eventually they all moved on to look for a hostel. Shortly after, I walked up to the Fortaleza, the impressive fortress that dominates the town and glowers across the river at Spain. I picked a restaurant on the western side and settled in the shade on the terrace for an indulgent lunch. A coal-seared half chicken was accompanied by salad, fried potatoes, rice and raw carrot, with water and a glass of vinho verde. A substantial meal but, unfortunately, the worst wine I had tasted so far – and I speak as someone who is very partial to vinho verde, normally one of Portugal's cleanest, most reliable and refreshing light wines. I finished with an espresso and paid €14, a steal for such a generous meal.

The sole waiter – an old style professional who clearly took great pride in his role – spent an inordinate amount of time discussing menu choices with his increasingly numerous clientele. I was astonished at how many queries could be raised and how much there was to discuss on the subject of salt cod!

After lunch I wandered past the Pousada, my dinner venue for the evening. Pousadas are the Portuguese equivalents of Spanish Paradores and are similarly government-owned, upmarket hotels, often found in historic palaces, monasteries or castles. I had stayed in quite a number of Paradores but had no experience of Pousadas. Despite a wonderful site commanding the river, the Valença establishment was an unfortunate melange of blocky, utilitarian modern additions to the original fortress that formed its core.

Moving on, I descended through a dark tunnel in the Fortaleza's fortifications, pursued by a squad of howling mountain bikers, delighting in the reverberations of their roars as they whizzed through the arches. Walking across the iron bridge over the river Miño/Minho, the border between Portugal and Spain, I promptly lost an hour of my life as the time changed to continental summertime.

Spain's anomalous choice of time zone is the result of a Fascist gesture of solidarity with Nazi-dominated Europe in 1940, when Franco switched his country from its 'natural' Greenwich Mean Time setting to Central European Time. The adverse consequences are particularly marked in Galicia, Spain's westernmost province, which shares much the same longitude as the centre and west of Ireland. In midwinter in Santiago de Compostela, for example, the sun sometimes doesn't rise until almost 9:00 am. By contrast Portugal, staying true to its longitude, keeps to GMT, in line with the UK.

It was now very hot and I was glad to spot a sign to the Parador. Staying in Paradores had become an enjoyable indulgence for Frances and me on our trips through Spain. We had sampled more than a dozen of them and Tui would be my first Parador experience without her. Sadly, the Tui establishment – a lumpen, granite pastiche of a Galician manor house – was not one of their more historic hotels, but it had a fine position in sweeping grounds looking out to the river and it promised a level of comfort above what I had known for the past five days. Admittedly, I had hardly endured penitential privations, but the prospect of a couple of nights in a massive bed in the muted hush of a gracious hotel fitted well with my plans for a mid-Camino break.

At Reception I requested a room with a bath and was assured that all the rooms had them. I was allocated a large corner room, lined with dark wood panelling. The almost equally spacious bathroom benefited from natural light streaming in through high stained glass windows – a rare delight in these days of windowless en suite cubicles. A deep, foaming bath washed the dirt of the road away while I reviewed my progress so far. I had walked 15.6 km that day, taking me to a total of 107 km since setting off from Porto on Sunday. According to John Brierley, 120 km remained to Santiago. It all seemed perfectly manageable.

New blisters had erupted on both feet, particularly the left, but, all in all, things were not too bad. I had coped well with the walking but felt no fitter – I still panted, open-mouthed, heart pounding, on the steeper inclines. And I probably hadn't lost any weight – this was perhaps hardly surprising in view of my beer consumption and the generous portions of the meals. But I felt really good and had no doubts about my stamina or my ability to finish the hike. In fact, I was enjoying it. Physically, if not spiritually, St James was doing me good.

After a satisfying bowlful of gin and tonic, I got the receptionist to call a taxi which took me back over the bridge to Portugal and my dinner date with Carolyn and Laurie.

The vehicle approach to the heart of the Fortaleza proved to be extremely convoluted and restrictive, policed by traffic lights at a succession of narrow arched gateways. Here the lights let some vehicles out, then allowed pedestrians to use the gateways free of traffic, and finally turned green for those of us queuing to drive in. It made for slow progress and eventually I opted to get out and walk. Even then, there was another light-controlled gateway to negotiate on foot. In their Pousada fastness, the ladies were clearly cutting no corners in their efforts to protect their virtue.

Arriving at the Pousada, which commanded a wonderful position high over the river, I found the Canadians on the bar terrace being buttonholed by a garrulous Englishwoman. She was recounting, in tiresome detail, the dash she and her husband had made from Bilbao or Santander, along northern Spain to Portugal, from where they were continuing on down to Faro to pick up their daughter and arrange for their son, who had just finished a shooting course with his cadet force, to join them and also a Canadian friend who was flying over and then they would move on to the Costa del Sol where they had a small holiday home and she had worked in Canada for a time and Santiago she had found disappointing and what a pity the cathedral (spoiler alert!) was all covered in scaffolding and bubblewrap and wasn't the Pousada a wonderful place and was the Prosecco Laurie and Carolyn were drinking the same as they had been given at the entrance when they arrived; was it any good?

The woman never drew breath, even when it became clear that her audience's expected guest had arrived. Needless to say I took an instant dislike to her, which came as a bit of a relief after six days bathed in brotherhood and bonhomie, with *'Bom Caminho'* and *'Buen Camino'* ringing in my ears. How good to be back – if briefly – in my familiar world of instant character judgment.

At this point, timing his arrival to take advantage of the tiniest glottal stop in his wife's outpouring, her husband arrived. With the satisfied air of a small town solicitor, he was exulting in the fact that, having crossed into Portugal, they were now back on 'English time'. Of course I scoffed at this but he insisted it had to be called 'English time', what with Greenwich and all that.

This was clearly the poor man's conversational high point of the evening because, quickly recovering from the unwarranted interruption for which he would no doubt pay a heavy price later, his unstanchable wife promptly renewed her logorrheaic flow. Clutching her Michelin road atlas, she proceeded to describe each of the multitude of split-second decisions she had had to make to navigate her hapless husband through the trials and tribulations of the motorways of Spain.

Fortunately, her ladyship now had to get on with planning the next stage of their journey, so she moved off across the terrace – not far enough away in my view – to begin laying the following day's roadside traps for her unfortunate spouse. My Hendricks and tonic couldn't have arrived at a better moment. Even though it cost an exorbitant €12.50 – more than twice the price of a G&T at the Parador – it was worth it.

Carolyn, Laurie and I eventually went into dinner in a room that offered equally superb views on to the Spanish side of the river. Back in England, a young Portuguese chef had insisted that I simply had to sample Pousada cuisine while I was in Portugal. The dining experience, he said, was much more rewarding than is sometimes endured in Spain's Paradores which can be institutional in their attitudes to service and are seldom praised for their cuisine. So I was very much looking forward to the meal.

Carolyn and Laurie seemed taken with the set menu so, for simplicity's sake but rather against my better judgement, I stuck with them. A simple starter of white asparagus and mayonnaise was acceptable but hardly exciting, while the main course of tuna steak was dull, dry and flavourless. What had happened to all those zingy Portuguese sauces?

We got through the meal with only a brief interruption from our fellow guest, by then installed at a nearby table. She sought advice on what to eat and quizzed each of us in turn as to what we'd had. Carolyn was happy to recommend the tuna and I confirmed that I had had it, but reserved any comment. Should she choose it, I was savouring the taste of an unworthy revenge – a rare blast of flavour in a banal repast.

The meal may have been poor but the company was good. Laurie and Carolyn proved to be delightful and interesting characters. As young women, both had travelled extensively in Europe, and Laurie, in particular, had led an amazingly varied life. A retired head teacher, she now lived part of the year in Mexico and worked with special needs children in an American school in Monterey – a job she clearly loved.

Previously she had held a Canadian government post, translating technical documents from Russian This was in the days of the Cold War and things became difficult when, through a shared interest in singing, Laurie befriended the wife of the Bulgarian ambassador who happened to be an opera singer. This harmless harmony across the great ideological divide spooked the spooks in Ottawa who quickly made it clear to Laurie that the friendship had to end.

Switching from Russian to French, Laurie then spent two years helping a friend set up a wine import business – a role in which she had enjoyed a good deal of bibulous hospitality in the homes of French wine producers. At some point she had also been a weaver, using Icelandic wool to produce waterproof jumpers and ponchos, and – to crown it all – was for a time the singer in a Rolling Stones tribute band.

Even as a head teacher, it seemed, Laurie had once 'taken the roof off the school' with a performance of Janis Joplin's 'Another Little Piece of my Heart'. According to Carolyn, Laurie possessed the best Janis Joplin voice since the much-lamented Miss Joplin herself. So very different from any head teacher I had ever known!

As it happened, Laurie and I shared a sad connection: her first husband had died of a brain tumour at 46, so she knew what Frances and I had been through. She had two sons and a daughter and was now married to a man from Louisiana who spent part of the year with her in Mexico and the rest of the time at their island cottage on Lake Ontario. Unfortunately, six weeks of rainfall had recently flooded the basement there, destroying many items Laurie had saved from her first marriage. This had clearly been a deeply distressing experience for her.

Carolyn was a good deal younger and had worked for a time as Laurie's deputy. A perky, energetic woman who was interested in everything, Carolyn seemed contently single and happy to host her 'children' – as she called her pupils – during the school day and just as happy to see them go home at the end of it. Very much a friends-oriented person, she made great play of her acquaintance, back in Canada, with a man from Cullybackey in Northern Ireland – a mere 40 miles from my home town, as she was delighted to show me on an iPhone app. We agreed this was clearly some form of near-miraculous connection between us.

They told me that, when we met that day in the church in Rates, I was the first person they had encountered on their Camino. They seemed so delighted to make my acquaintance that I felt I could only eventually disappoint by being insufficiently interesting. Certainly my timid life could never stand comparison with Laurie's.

After a jovial evening without further interruptions from the maddening anglo-navigatrix, a muscle-bound taxi driver, who texted all the way to the Spanish border, whipped me back to the Parador. The fare was €7 – less than on the way there –

but when I handed over a €10 note, the driver made great play of scratching and scraping for change while the cab sat in the floodlights outside the hotel. In a better mood I might have told him to keep the odd Euros but I was pissed off with him for texting while driving and so determined to extract my change.

After what seemed ages he handed me an astonishing pile of grubby coins with a curt 'I'm sorry'. I thought: 'you bastard, you're gaming this' and searched through the brown mound for anything of value. There was one 50 cent piece in a pile of fives, tens and twenties. I withdrew about 70 cents and handed the rest back to him.

Based on his 'I'm sorry', I said: 'Do you speak English?'

'A little,' he replied.

'Well, your passengers would be a lot happier if you stopped texting when you're driving.'

With that, I got out of the cab, feeling disgruntled. The incident probably didn't reflect well on either of us but, on Sunday, I would, once again, wrap myself in the Camino's mantle of meekness. Just then, it felt good to be briefly riveted back into my natural curmudgeonly carapace.

Saturday 15 July

Tui

Examining evacuation plans in hotel bedrooms has been a sad habit of mine ever since I endured a brief period of employment as a management trainee with Marks & Spencer in the 1970s. Each time we stayed in a hotel on company business, we were required not just to check but actually walk the fire escape route from our room. We also had to keep a torch by the bedside to help us find our way through smoke. Though I worked for the company for only seven months, this awareness of escape routes had stayed with me, but I didn't actually walk the routes any more.

While studying the evacuation plan in my Parador bedroom, I was pleased to note that my room was a good deal

larger than the others along the corridor. I had no idea why –
other than by my obvious virtue as a pilgrim – I merited the
distinction of larger quarters. I just hoped it wouldn't be
reflected in an increased bill when I checked out.

After a restful night in my unaccustomed space, with no
need to find the fire exit, I headed down for my first Parador
breakfast without Frances. Breakfasts in Parador hotels are
normally excellent and today's presented the usual generous
and varied spread. I surprised myself by opting for a fine
selection of fruit before resorting to a more predictable
combination of fried egg, tortilla, chorizo sausage and what
passed for bacon in these parts.

Of course something had to mar the experience and, as was
often the case, it was the dreaded piped music. Having crossed
the border, I had left the realm of Portuguese *fado* behind – I
can happily handle blues in the morning – but I could have
been mollified by a selection of jaunty Galician folk tunes. No
such luck. Today's aural earwax was constipated lift music at its
worst – the sort that farts out banal, aborted phrases and then
simply repeats them without any development, motion or
delivery. It just hung there, stuck – probably originally
scratched out by a straining, egg-bound journeyman. One day,
perhaps, I would have the largeness of soul to ignore such
rubbish but that day still seemed a long way off.

After breakfast I worked on a poem that I realised had been gestating in my head as a major part of the process of saying farewell to Frances. Before leaving home I had jotted down ideas and disjointed phrases with the vague notion that, at some point, I would deal with Frances's death in a poem. It made sense to me to do so and I quickly settled into the work

The town's pleasant riverfront was really an elongated park and well used by strollers, runners and parents with children. I sat on a shady bench beside trees whose lower trunks were wrapped in what I assumed was Morning Glory but, given my botanical ignorance, could well have been something else. I found myself in an emotional state but realised it was necessary to facilitate what I was attempting to write. In some strange, cathartic way, I could even have been enjoying the release of my feelings. It certainly kept me working on the poem.

I recalled something Carolyn had asked me the previous evening. She wanted to know what gift I would buy myself as a memento of the Camino. She had been very taken with a bracelet that Simone had been wearing. It had miniatures of all the emblems of the Camino attached to it: scallop shell, wayside arrows and so on. I said I didn't really indulge in such souvenirs but she pressed me – Carolyn is a very direct interrogator and, I'm sure, an effective, no-nonsense teacher when called upon.

Without hesitation, as I had had the idea for some time, I said that, somewhere along the Camino, I would pick up a stone and bring it back to place on Frances's grave. I had already done this in January after I revisited St Jeannet, a hill town above Nice in Provence, where we had once spent a family holiday.

Frances had always brought back stones – sometimes full-size rocks – from places we visited. In Australia, she had even taken a small amount of red soil from near Uluru: a cardinal cultural and ecological sin I felt sure. I had decided I would only bring her stones from revisits to places we had previously shared and Santiago – if not actually the Portuguese Camino – fitted the bill, thanks to our visit in 1994. Carolyn and Laurie both agreed that bringing back a stone was a fitting idea.

Now, sitting beside the Minho, I began to think of my poem as a present from the Camino. I resolved to get it into shape so that I could at least let Carolyn and Laurie have a copy as my gift to them for their companionship along the Way.

All this kept me in a fairly rheumy-eyed state, sitting by the peaceful river and looking across at Portugal. I was surprised when I noticed how much time had elapsed. I had better stop and take a look at Tui before the day was too far gone. And I realised I would soon need to head towards licensed premises, if only for a renewed supply of paper serviettes. But my stomach was also noisily telling me that, despite the leap to Spanish time, lunch was overdue.

Tui is a happily aged town of mellow stone and, as I climbed up into it, the old quarter added to the good impression made by the riverfront. The streets were surprisingly quiet, so clearly tourists weren't scouring through the place in the heat of July.

I settled for lunch in a *jamoneira* – a restaurant specialising in the many varieties of Spanish ham. It stood just across from the main cathedral entrance which featured carved dark wood doors framed by a lavishly decorated stone arch. Unfortunately, a makeshift line of pilgrim's laundry, strung below the first floor windows of a nearby hostel, rather defeated the dignified effect. As I had frequently demonstrated myself, twenty-first century pilgrims set more store by clean, dry hiking gear than cleansing their immortal souls.

My first intention had been to work my way through some lovely Bellota ham – this was a *jamoneira*, after all – but I was quickly distracted by mention of anchovies and peppers on the menu. The actual dish proved disappointing: pequillo peppers with anchovies, pinned on a layer of dull plastic cheese which had in turn expired on hard, dry toast. But a generous mixed salad with tuna, white asparagus and deliciously sweet tomatoes (not one of them green) redeemed things a little.

To reprise my earlier musical preoccupations for a moment, a selection of what I could only assume were *zarzuela* tunes was playing in the background. *Zarzuela* is a particularly Spanish form of operetta with which I could claim no familiarity. These were certainly light opera numbers I didn't recognise but they had the strutting, overblown 'look at me singing' tone that I imagined *zarzuela* required. I confess I rather liked them and, indeed, probably enjoyed the piped music more than the meal. Very perverse, I'm sure, given my breakfast time rant. Ah well, few things in life are more constant than inconsistency.

After lunch I wandered round the sleepy town. The day had grown decidedly hot but, as the shops were closed, there was no way I'd be able to find the quality notepaper I had decided to seek out on which to inscribe copies of my poem for Carolyn and Laurie. I drifted back along the river and spent what remained of the afternoon relaxing in the cool of my dark-panelled room. I even slept for a while. When I woke, I ran a bath – my second in 24 hours and third for the year: a record for the millennium.

Downstairs, as the sun moved away from the terrace, a welcome wind blew up from the river. I settled at a table with the first of two Tanqueray gins, raising my glass each time to the smiling lady who had introduced me to the stuff.

By this point – to reprise another theme – I was getting just a little anxious about my laundry. Shortly after my arrival the previous day I had entrusted a bundle of my kit to a smiling room service woman on the clear understanding that it would be returned by about five the next day. It was now nine o'clock but, when I popped up to my room, there was still no sign of my socks, t-shirts and precious hi-tech underwear.

Most of these sporting gear items, I noticed, had copious instructions on their labels about what was required – and what not to do – when laundering them. So, as I handed them over, I emphasised the need for just a simple wash or rinse. Who would have thought that looking so naff brought with it so much responsibility?

I presented myself at Reception to make inquiries but, before I could say anything, with a dramatic sweep of her arms, the smiling receptionist handed me an elegant wicker basket in which all my hi-tech unmentionables lay neatly folded in full view. My face must have been a picture of delight. Hiking, it seems, makes washerfolk of us all.

At what I considered the acceptably Spanish hour of 9:30 I wandered into the dining room in search of dinner. At first I thought the place was deserted but I soon discovered my fellow guests were seated in a cool, glassed-in space beyond the main room that offered superb views on to the river.

Padrón peppers – again! – and, once more, not a flicker of heat. These were followed by eight baby scallops in their shells: tiny offerings to St James. Far from replete, I ordered pork ribs, which arrived with salad, peppers and roast potatoes. All in all, a rather indulgent meal and much more flavoursome than the previous evening's offering at the Pousada.

At some point I realised I was the only person in the dining room who was wearing shorts. Everyone else was smartly dressed and – most unusual in my experience of Paradores – all my fellow diners were Spanish. Perhaps the gruesome Brexit *auto da fe* currently taking place back in the UK was already having an effect on Brits' forays abroad.

At 11:00, four Spanish men arrived, clearly expecting to have dinner, but they were swiftly sent on their way. Maybe even Spaniards are beginning to realise that an hour before midnight is indeed a mighty strange time to begin one's evening meal.

Frances Farewell

In memory of my wife
Frances Hamblin

For Maeve, Hannah, Conor

I

I stand at the foot of your hi-tech bed,
Six feet between us – the distance is vast.
You, silent on the edge of death, finding
Your way to your ending. In this room where
Gladly you blessed family and friends with meals
Oiled and flavoured by your generous soul.

II

I spent too long in the garden that day,
Talking to your old schoolfriends, dallying
In the sunshine while, inexorably,
Indoors your life force ebbed. In the end
No one was with you. You found your way alone.

III

I woke at four – the monitor silent.
No breath, no sound – I knew. You lay on your
Side as we'd left you, a few bubbles of
Spit round your lips. Clammy, stiffening, cold.
I moved you on to your back, arranged
Your hair. One eye stubbornly half-open,
A hint of your mother's withering glance.
Oh my poor girl. After six hard years
It's happened. I pad round the rooms of my
Motherless children, whispering:
'She's gone. Mummy's gone.'

IV

And of course the sun came out for you that
Bright September day when we carried you
Suntanned to your grave. Pillowed on lavender
And freesia, no waxen pallor, no hue-drained
Shroud for you. A flowing, floral dress,
Just slightly faded – and barefoot as you
Loved to be, on warm sand or dewy grass
In sun-kissed Mediterranean days.

V

Floating, floral dresses suited you well.
I brought one to you once in Mageloup –
Vivid, brash roses, tight bodice, full skirt.
My risky choice. You loved it – and sitting
By the Miño, I see you in it still,
Drifting through sunflowers beside the Gironde.

VI

I stand at the foot of your open grave,
Six feet between us – the distance is vast.
Your basketwork coffin, latticed with roses,
Bedded beyond Warblington's crumbling tower.
Stumbling I offer my paltry farewell.

'Goodnight sweetheart.
May sweet flowers blossom where you lie
And colours soar to meet the sky.
Goodbye, goodbye, goodbye.'

Camino Portugués
July 2017

Movements II
Tui to Santiago de Compostela

Sunday 16 July

Tui to Porriño

It was the start of my second week on the Camino but, first, a good Parador breakfast was in order. Having finally remembered the Earl Grey teabags I had been carrying in my rucksack since Porto, I was disappointed to learn that my hopes of a proper cup of tea were threatened by a power cut. After explaining that there was *'no luz'*, one of the waiting staff took charge and, accepting my teabag with good grace, returned, somehow, with bergamot-infused liquor. At least the lack of power put paid to any piped music to mar the start of the day.

Pleased that my amply proportioned accommodation had incurred no extra charge, I left the hotel just before nine and headed along the riverbank in a welcome morning breeze. This was a much more pleasant and direct stroll than the official Camino route which wound up through the town, past the cathedral. I preferred walking beside the river and, anyway, I had covered most of the historic route during my wanderings about town the previous day.

A fully dressed Portuguese naval vessel – clearly on a courtesy visit – was moored at the Spanish Navy post at the end of the riverside walk. It had replaced a Spanish gunboat that had occupied the same spot the previous day. The thought of naval gunboats patrolling the peaceful Minho in our open Europe of no borders seemed somewhat incongruous.

I turned up the hill and on to the Camino proper. The day promised an easy 18 km or so hike with no particular climbs. And, while no doubt pleasant enough, this stage lacked the challenge of the tougher hilly sections. I had enjoyed my day off but it felt good to be back on the Way. Each day on the Camino was a day with a purpose, even if it was only to reach a designated spot and make a little more progress across the map. And, after a day on my own in Tui, it would be good to bump into fellow Caministas again.

The walking may have been gentle but, as I was soon to discover, it traversed a war zone. As about two thirds of the day's stage was on roadway, the Camino organisation had opened up an alternative green lane option to avoid part of the section through the town of Porriño. This cut out what seemed to be a grim, if more direct, trudge through the industrial outskirts of the town, past an area that specialised in quarrying, cutting and preparing granite – heavy industry by anyone's standards.

Business owners on the original route had not taken kindly to this development and had retaliated. They had obliterated signs for the alternative green route, mostly by tarring over them. They had replaced them with yellow arrows encouraging walkers to continue straight on, presumably past their premises. According to John Brierley, this sort of thing had been a feature of the Camino since medieval days: not surprisingly, everyone en route wanted a cut of the *peregrinos'* pennies. As the day's stage had already proved a good deal less charming than many previous sections, I was more than happy to take the longer, green route.

As I arrived at St Campio, a hamlet about five kilometres from Porriño, a religious fiesta was getting under way. In a plaza in front of a small chapel, a brass band, featuring a flurry of competitive trumpeters, was performing on a large stage. Gaudy banners were ranged in front of it and these were soon joined by a cart filled with votive candles in windproof holders.

In front of the stage, three objects of particular veneration attracted straggles of the faithful. There was a small Madonna-like figure, a statue of a Franciscan monk and – the obvious star of the show – a recumbent, painted saint lying on a carved wood bier under an ornate four-poster bed-like canopy.

These figures were targets for frequent wiping, stroking and kissing – and not just by devout old women. I watched one man wipe the faces of all three with his handkerchief before stuffing it back in his pocket. Perhaps the poor chap was suffering from a bad case of hay fever and had lost all faith in antihistamines.

A large beer tent had been erected for the event, so it clearly wasn't going to be all holy Joery. I sampled my first Estrella of the trip and fell into conversation with a young couple from Murcia who had begun their Camino from Tui that day. The city is a popular starting point for pilgrims who just want to cover the minimum mileage needed to earn their *Compostela*. It was the woman's first Camino, but her companion had previously cycled the *Francés* from Leon to Santiago.

The young couple left some time before me but, when I set out, I caught up with them embarrassingly quickly. I hoped they didn't think I was stalking them. We walked together for a while and I found myself saying that, for young people, they walked very slowly. Once we reached the green diversion which meandered along a riverside path, I began to pull away. I simply couldn't restrict myself to their pace.

Encounters with fellow hikers over the previous week had convinced me that I was probably one of the faster pacers along the Camino – particularly when compared with those carrying a full pack, complete with camping and cooking gear. Perhaps it was down to the hours I had spent marching along Roman road XIX like a demented legionary hoping to gain promotion by catching the centurion's eye.

Once in Porriño I headed for the unpromising-looking, brown-tiled bulk of the Parque Hotel. Despite its lack of airs and graces, it offered a perfectly adequate room for €40 which I paid upfront. This meant I could shoot off in the morning without breakfast (which, when I enquired, wasn't offered anyway) to get a start on the steep climb and descent between Porriño and Redondela.

Porriño didn't appear to be sharpening the cutting edge of Galician gastronomy or, if it were, the natives were keeping the good places well concealed. I did a full *paseo* of the main entertainment and restaurant area, which amounted to about a street and a half in the pedestrianised centre. All that was available were indistinguishable café restaurants offering pizza, pasta and local dishes. I sampled one of these outlets at lunchtime, with mixed results. Though hungry, I couldn't quite bring myself to eat some chillingly albino chicken that resembled larger versions of my Compeed blister plasters.

For my evening meal I had little choice but to opt for an establishment just along from my lunch venue that offered similar fare. The place was humming with customers but no one was eating – they were all just drinking, smoking and chatting. I was lucky to get an outside table but it had the inevitable drawback. The Spanish remain heroic smokers – particularly, for some reason, their women. I was sat downwind from one chain-smoking *señora* who was doggedly lighting her next cigarette as soon as the previous one finished. Her dainty shoes formed the centrepiece of a constellation of butts on the paviours.

It's easy to forget how disgusting a habit smoking now appears. How did we remain so addicted for so long? And how dramatic has the change been since the legislation passed? But whatever the undoubted health benefits to the populace, in Spain at least, a heavy gastronomic price has been paid. Forcing smokers out of doors has, I'm sure, caused a marked loss of flavour in the hams that hang from the ceilings of bars right across the country. Previously these were gratuitously and pungently kippered by the dense smoke rising from drinkers' cigarettes. Today's smoke-free, air-conditioned clarity offers no such tangy bonus. But nothing has yet extinguished the fug on the terraces – something that can make dining *al fresco* in Spain very unpleasant at times.

When I requested a Galician beer from my large, jovial host, he promised an Estrella but produced a darker version in a 1906 Special Reserva glass. I was delighted to find that, compared to the amarillo lagers I had previously been guzzling, this actually had taste and flavour. At last my prayers had been answered: this was a minor miracle on the Camino.

A second beer was soon required but, having requested Estrella again, I was crestfallen when a young waiter produced what could only be the usual lager variant. I queried the difference between this and my previous beer but he assured me it was the same.

I was unconvinced and, when a woman at a nearby table was served a maroon beer, I called the waiter over to point out the difference between it and my urine-tinted nectar. He again maintained it was the same beer – just a different glass – but, moments later, he shot out of the bar and, without a word, scooped up my beer and vanished back inside.

Perhaps he was simply going to decant it into the other type of glass just to show me... but, no: he quickly reappeared, apologising profusely, and handed me a 1906 Grande Reserva glass of brownish ale. This was indeed the stuff I had been savouring. Here was sweet victory in an international, bilingual beer standoff. I sipped my 1906 with deep appreciation and decided it was indeed a very good year.

Sitting by myself in a bar full of people all happily drinking, talking and laughing, brought home to me that the times I had felt most alone since Frances's death were those occasions when I was surrounded by people. I had spent much of my time on the Camino walking by myself and had enjoyed it immensely. I had never felt alone. Loneliness and solitude were very different conditions – and I was at ease with solitude. But, sitting at a table by myself, amidst the hum of chattering, laughing people, I felt alone. Loneliness, like Sartre's hell, is other people.

Monday 17 July

Porriño to Arcade

Despite a hot and stuffy night, I slept well, with the window open but a blessed absence of mosquitoes. With no breakfast on offer, I rose early to hit the road. But first, my daily pre-hike preparations had to be observed. By now these had taken on the characteristics and fixed nature of a morning ritual. Perhaps I should describe the occult and sacred ceremony in some detail.

The process began with that essential emollient: Vaseline. This was, without doubt, the Heineken of the hike: the substance that reached the parts one might otherwise prefer not to reach. It was applied in generous quantities to intimate places to prevent chafing – in the groin, the perineum and between the butt cheeks. Chafing is the great enemy of the hiker – and an especial terror for males. Following this, everything else down there was liberally dusted with medicated talcum powder. Then, and only then, could the hi-tech Swiss boxer shorts be donned. These were designed to do many things – at least according to the copywriter's effusions on their substantial packaging. One of the key features, as an experienced trekker friend explained when recommending them for my Camino, was an inverted triangle of fabric bands just above the buttock crack. These ensured that no sweat leached down into said crevice. Who knew such things existed? But, even on the hottest day, the pants seemed to be effective. Well worth £30 of anyone's money, I'd say.

Of course, once these highly engineered athletic garments were dragged into position over my beer-loving anatomy and any appendages consigned to their rightful place within them, the effect was utterly unlike the thrusting, sculpted photographs on the expensive packaging. Still, any amount of body shaming was a price worth paying to avoid being chafed.

My arthritic left knee needed all the help it could get and this was provided by an elasticated wrap-round support, reassuringly branded 'Ultimate Performance'. This had a circular hole in the front that allowed my kneecap to move freely. However, the effect was to make it look as though I was wearing a gimp mask on my leg or a helpful target guide for an anatomically ignorant IRA punishment squad. But the support proved effective and minimised any swelling round the knee – something that occasionally happened after a long hike.

Next, the vitally important area of feet. Here, despite what I considered a vast investment of £80 in bespoke insoles, individually heat-moulded to the shape of each foot, I had been dealing with blisters, hot spots, blackening toenails and much more that merited attention. But the main focus was blisters, of which I had one of a fairly hardy nature at the back of my right heel and at least three on my left foot. One of these was not a problem, however, and the original blister on the inside of the foot, caused by one of those expensive but ill-fitting insoles (quickly discarded), had hardened up nicely. I just had to cover the hard one with a Compeed plaster to prevent anything new kicking off. The other, on the outer edge of the foot, remained a bother. The original blister had been joined by one immediately behind but, fortunately, a Compeed plaster was just about capable of covering both.

When they heard I was having problems with blisters, my kind Canadian friends supplied me with additional plasters and sterile alcohol swabs. The latter had proved very useful to sterilise the needle from the sewing kit provided in my Parador bathroom. I was aware that piercing blisters and expelling the contents was not the approved methodology but, at this point, I was simply looking at ways to ensure my feet took up less space in my tight-fitting shoes.

After Compeed and anything else had been applied, I filled my socks for the day with a generous snowstorm of medicated talcum powder before easing my feet into my virulent, hi-vis striped running shoes. I had had my doubts about these, but they were very light and had proved remarkably suitable for the dry conditions. I was certainly glad not to be plodding along in the chunky walking boots I normally preferred.

Once all these ministrations were complete, it was a fairly simple task to don whatever wicking, flicking, quick-dry lightweight sports top and shorts I would be inflicting on the Camino faithful that day. As I was walking mostly with the sun on my back, a wide-brimmed sun hat and something called a buff – a soft cylinder of lightweight material designed to protect the neck and exposed skin round the collar from sunburn – were essential.

Finally, I grabbed my two most reliable companions on the road – my Leki walking poles. Given the rickety state of both my knees, these were utterly essential. In recent years, my left knee had developed a degree of osteoarthritis and, not to be outdone, the right one occasionally joined in with creaks and cracks of its own. Needless to say, I attributed their decrepitude not to my increased age but to hours kneeling, as an altar boy, on cold marble floors before my childish limbs were properly formed. Where would we apostates be without the Church to blame for our physical and psychological shortcomings?

The poles were a great help, especially on gradients where they took a lot of weight off my knees. But they also helped propel me along on the flatter stretches. The Nordic walking rhythm of using all four limbs really suited me and the poles provided additional thrust that kept me bowling along at what I felt was a healthy pace.

At 7:30, suitably greased and armoured, I stepped out into a cooler, grey day, with low cloud and mist hanging in the valleys. The sun was doing its best to break through but, for the moment, the cooler air made for ideal walking conditions.

I found the Camino easily and almost immediately fell in with a smiling woman from Rome. She too had done the *Camino Francés* and wasn't impressed with the Portuguese version, particularly the signposting and expense. This surprised me but, for once, I held my peace.

Before long she accused me of running rather than walking and it was a fair point. I liked to get in a first hour of fairly vigorous walking – the previous day I had clocked just over five kilometres in the first 60 minutes which, with a full pack, I considered respectable. I didn't think I would meet or exceed that achievement on this stretch, as we were due to hit a hilly section rather early in the day.

When the *bella signora* stopped to photograph some Camino signage she clearly found wanting, I parted company with her and hared along, walking poles thwacking – the very Jimmy Edwards of Caministas.

The walk led uphill to a pleasant little settlement called Mos which boasted a Camino souvenir shop and a café. In anticipation of finally filling my current notebook, I bought a handsome blue replacement graced by a yellow Camino arrow on the cover.

Next I dropped into Café Flora for coffee and a *tostada* smeared with tomato pulp and olive oil. This was an adequate breakfast and it felt good to have covered some distance before indulging. A grey-bearded man, roughly my own age, greeted me at the counter as he waited to pay. He engaged in badinage in Spanish with (I assumed) the eponymous Flora and a large local lady who was propped up on a stool in the corner. I was sure I understood him to say that he was interested in learning Gallego – the language of Galicia – as well as speaking Spanish. As he left I wished him a good Camino in English.

After Mos, it was steep going, onwards and upwards through the misty countryside, with birds singing and the sun beginning to break through. I caught up with my fellow grey beard who turned out to be a voluble barrister from Sydney. Like so many of my fellow walkers, Godfrey too had previously walked the *Francés* and had clearly been infected with the Camino bug. He was already planning his next hike: tackling the *Via Podensis*, a feeder route to the *Camino Francés* that runs from Le Puy-en-Velay in the Haute-Loire in France to the Pyrenees. It sounded an interesting option; perhaps I'd think about it for a future adventure.

As I had suspected, Godfrey was a keen linguist – hence his interest in Gallego – and spoke an impressive number of languages. Though he could no doubt afford to stay in hotels, he preferred to take his chances in pilgrim hostels. This allowed him to practise his linguistic skills with fellow pilgrims from around the world – something he found little opportunity to do in Sydney.

Describing one of the more unpleasant aspects of his experience on the *Camino Francés*, Godfrey became very exercised about people who used the Camino as an outdoor lavatory, littering hedges and ditches with wind-blown scraps of used toilet paper. In his opinion, the culprits were mostly young people. Why couldn't they control their bowels, he asked? Why didn't they respect the Camino and the planet?

I had heard about this unsightly business on stretches of the *Camino Francés*, but I couldn't help wondering which had the greater impact on the planet: some slowly decaying if rather disgusting paper or the carbon footprint of a hiker flying from the southern hemisphere year after year to walk the byways of Iberia and France? But, for the second time that day, I held my peace. I have found it best not to engage in verbal sparring with barristers, unless required to do so in a court of law.

While I was unwilling to confront Godfrey's scatological *bête noire*, I was myself on the case of a different ecological crime: I was on the hunt for the Phantom Flosser. Over the previous few days I had noticed a number of small, plastic-handled dental floss picks discarded on the Camino. Some oral hygiene obsessive was clearly flossing as he or she walked along and calmly tossing these annoying little objects on the ground when done. I found it very objectionable.

Funnily enough, Carolyn and Laurie had also noticed the wretched things and shared my distaste at seeing these egregious little items so blithely strewn along our path. It was as much as we could do to stop ourselves acquiring some DNA and forming a posse to hunt down the halitosis-haunted malefactor. Indeed, for some days I found myself eyeing the gleaming smiles of fellow pilgrims with suspicion in the hope that I might be able to identify the culprit. With any luck it would turn out to be a French person so that I could righteously confront them and yell: '*J'accuse*'.

Leaving aside our bugbears, Godfrey and I continued to chat happily as we passed over the high point for the day and dropped down into the busy town of Redondela. Godfrey wanted to buy bread, ham and tomatoes with the intention of lunching somewhere along the way. He invited me to join him but I decided to carry on a bit further. It was only 11:00 and I wanted to walk some more. I moved on through the town and started the next section towards Pontevedra, my destination for the following night.

After consulting the guidebook, I decided to aim for Arcade. This would allow me to spend a night by the sea and reduce the distance for the following day to a mere 16 km. This meant I could make the most of my stopover at the Parador in Pontevedra, where I had already booked a room.

After Redondela, a further climb was indicated but I stopped before this for lunch at the unprepossessing Jumboli, *Pensión Rústica*, a roadside restaurant right on the busy N550. With lorries and cars hurtling by, it wasn't the most picturesque of locations but it provided an excellent lunch.

My capacity to consume a substantial lunch – accompanied by one or two beers – had been remarked on by some of my fellow hikers. They declared they would simply fall asleep if they indulged in a large midday meal or a couple of beers. But I looked forward to my lunch break. It was an important part of what had developed into a pleasing rhythm for each day: set off without a meal; walk two hours, then have breakfast; walk a couple more hours, then a coffee stop; a couple of hours later, lunch; then, after a few more hours, perhaps a beer stop before finally arriving at one's destination for the night.

Of course, when I made good progress, days often finished early, so the late afternoon beer stop might coincide with arrival at my hotel. But the pattern of the day made for easy, episodic walking and, after a halt, I never found it difficult to shoulder my rucksack and carry on.

The welcoming Jumboli provided vegetable soup followed by succulent, corn-fed chicken of a deep saffron yellow. This was accompanied by a generous amount of Padrón peppers and potatoes. By now I had consumed more than a hundred Padrón peppers in various places and not one had offered even the tiniest tingle of heat. Come Thursday, when I would reach the town of Padrón, after which these cold-hearted capsicums were named, questions would have to be asked.

I declined the *postre* that was included with the menu but accepted a coffee. I also had a large bottle of water (to recharge one of my rucksack vessels) and two Estrella 1906s – my new, approved beer of the Camino. All this came to €9.50 – value we could only dream of in England.

While I was tucking into my meal, I saw Godfrey cross the N550 and continue along the Camino. He was carrying a Dia supermarket bag with his lunch provisions and I noticed he was limping slightly.

Lunch finished, I crossed the N550 and began a steep climb through eucalyptus woodland towards the high point of the stage to Pontevedra. Already that summer, the central part of Portugal had suffered terrifying forest fires with dozens of fatalities. With their high oil content, eucalyptus trees were notoriously volatile, exploding into torches of flame should a wildfire reach them. While I had yet to hear of any wildfires in Galicia, since the start of my hike, whenever I walked through eucalyptus groves, my ears were pricked for the crackle and pop of anything resembling a fire. So far, there had been no reason to worry but, in the intense July heat, it seemed sensible to stay alert.

An old man appeared, shuffling along slowly with the help of a stick. Well wrapped up in cardigan and sensible hat, despite the sun having finally burned off the mist, he was clearly a local out for a stroll,. He stopped me and started talking about Gallego and I was sure he said he had met an Australian who was interested in the language. I told him I knew the chap he was talking about and apologised for not having any of the language. Nevertheless, we made a gallant attempt at a conversation before we went our separate ways. I felt sure that hailing random hikers provided the old chap with welcome entertainment on quiet afternoons, but I wondered how many could stretch to an exchange in Gallego.

Shortly after this encounter I began to catch glimpses of sea through the trees and gradually a beautiful vista of a blue water inlet opened out. This was the Ría de Vigo, the first of the picturesque inlets that slice up the southwestern coast of Galicia. After days of inland walking, I found myself surprisingly moved to be within reach of the sea.

Checking the guidebook again, I identified what appeared to be a waterfront hotel in Arcade, with the added bonus of a Michelin-recommended fish restaurant just a short distance from it. I decided to make these my target for the evening. The day seemed to be promising a good ending.

Towards the bottom of the descent I caught up with Godfrey and we walked into Arcade together. I outlined my dinner plans but Godfrey said he was too tired to appreciate a Michelin-starred restaurant (I wasn't sure it was starred: just listed as worth trying). But he indicated he might join me for a beer once he had had a sleep in his hostel.

After we passed the Hotel Duarte, which had been my original choice for the night until I had been seduced by the potential charms of the waterfront option, Godfrey peeled off for his hostel. He was desperate to stay ahead of a gang of singing Serbs – one with a large national flag swinging from his rucksack – whom we had passed a few minutes earlier.

I carried on down into the town and followed the main road to my new hotel. I had tried to contact them earlier by phone but had no response – not a good sign. And, sure enough, the hotel was closed for renovation – or *'reformas'* as the notice in Spanish informed me. This was a blow, but the building was in a horrible position, right beside the busy bridge that carried the N550 over the river. The small town was clearly a bottleneck, with long lines of lorries backed up in both directions.

Worse was to come. The Michelin-recommended Arcadia restaurant was, as I feared it might be, closed on Mondays. There was nothing for it but to trudge back up through the town to the Duarte, but not before I phoned to make sure they had a room for me. I paid the receptionist the required €25 and set off up to the first floor, not expecting very much – though I noticed that the Duarte had doubled its stars from one to two since its mention in Mr Brierley's guidebook.

Not only did my room turn out to be fine, with a perfectly good bathroom, but both bedroom and bathroom windows provided excellent views on to the sea. My prospects had certainly improved.

After removing my shoes, I was horrified to see that a large new blister – very red and looking for all the world like a blood blister – had erupted just above one of the existing extrusions on my left foot. This was disturbing and I couldn't understand why it should have appeared there, except that I had inserted a cotton wool pad into my sock over the existing blister in the hope of easing any friction. Perhaps the pad had somehow curled up and rubbed up this new injury.

I admit I am not the most body-aware of people, but it still amazed me how I could walk quite a distance and only really become aware of damage to my feet when I took off my shoes. I decided to remove the Compeed pad – not always the easiest of manoeuvres as they are very sticky and there was a risk of peeling off skin and so making matters worse. After a shower I lay back with my left foot raised on my rucksack. I wasn't sure there was much else I could do at this point as, after consulting Dr Internet, I decided not to follow my instinct to lance and drain the thing.

After a while, feeling the inevitable need for a beer, I limped gingerly down the stairs. The hotel bar was on the ground floor with open patio seating just across the road. Both commanded lovely views of the inlet. It was a beautiful, warm evening and the sun would soon begin to sink towards the horizon. Perhaps I could look forward to seeing a dramatic

Galician sunset reflected through the warm tones of a 1906 Grand Reserva? This was perfect. Why go anywhere else?

Alas, when I indicated to the receptionist that I would like to avail myself of the bar's finest offerings, she informed me it was closed – Monday was the staff's rest day. I whinged like hell that I had walked 23 km that day and didn't want to stagger any further just for a drink. Why couldn't she just open the bar? She wasn't exactly run off her feet. Hordes of hobbling pilgrims weren't piling through the door. But she was immovable. What a way to run a hospitality business!

When I asked her to recommend a bar nearby, she produced a map and marked a couple of options. One, she assured me, was even an actual 'pub' – whatever that meant in Galicia. Of course, this would involve tramping all the way back into town but there was no option. Collecting a walking pole to take the weight off my sore left foot, I was a far from happy bunny as I hirpled back down the road.

Predictably, the promised pub was firmly shut, as was the other seafood restaurant mentioned in the guide which had been my fallback for dinner. In fact, the restaurant wasn't just closed – it was for sale. And nearly every other outlet connected with food or drink in the wretched town seemed to be shut. Arcade was proving to be no arcadia; I was rapidly going off the place.

Eventually I found a stall in a café beside the N550 and settled down to enjoy a welcome bottle of 1906 amid the fumes of passing juggernauts. I was part way through a second bottle when my hostess began pulling down the metal shutters. It was, it seemed, closing time – at 6:30! What the hell was going on? Was early closing one of the ways Galicians distinguished themselves from Spaniards?

I asked if there was a restaurant somewhere – anywhere – that might possibly be open but the landlady didn't hold out much hope. She shut up shop and left me to finish my beer on her forecourt. By this time I had had enough of the combination of diesel fumes and the smell of hot, dry seaweed coming off the shoreline at low tide, so I headed further into the interior of the disobliging town.

Nothing filled me with hope. A hungry night seemed inevitable unless I settled for cake and ice cream which appeared to be all that was on offer. So much for the famed Galician seafood that I had been so looking forward to. Eventually I found a bar and comforted myself with another 1906. Little by little I began to mellow and, idly reading the label, realised why I might like Estrella's finest so much and why it appeared to have so much more flavour than other beers hereabouts. The alcohol content was 6.5%! Just this once, perhaps, a liquid repast would suffice.

Tuesday 18 July

Arcade to Pontevedra

Almost inevitably, morning in Arcade dawned grey and overcast. What else could the poor town do? This was the first day I felt no need of sunglasses or hat. I left the hotel at 8:30, dropped down into the town and almost immediately found Carolyn and Laurie breakfasting at a street corner café. They had just spent a relaxing day off the trail at a resort hotel on the coast. So, after my similar stopover in Tui, our Camino sequences had realigned.

I joined them for a humble pilgrim's *tostada* with butter and marmalade. Though I had only just started walking, the blisters on my left foot were already hurting, so I took off my sock and spent some time sorting things out. Normally, I wouldn't think of baring my feet in a public refreshment facility but I felt sure the clientele in cafés along the Camino were more than inured to this sort of exposure. They had probably seen a good deal worse.

Rejigging my footwear seemed to help, so we set off together towards the beautiful old bridge that spans the Rio Verdugo. I stopped to let Carolyn take my photograph – an offer that pleased me. I have yet to develop the self-reflective habit of the selfie, so, up to that point, I had no visual record of myself in full hiking regalia.

Across the river, the Camino rose up along steep stony paths and I became aware that I wouldn't be able to continue to walk at Carolyn and Laurie's somewhat gentler pace. So I made my excuses and shot off, poles flying. Later Carolyn sent me a brief video of my disappearing back with the message: 'You do move quickly, Patrick'.

I had said I would wait for them at the top of the hill but the climb proved to be surprisingly long and hard – equal to if not more testing than the previous day's ascent which had been so grimly flagged up in the guidebook. And this despite the fact it was only 125 metres against yesterday's 145. Perhaps the apparent difficulty was due to the state of my feet.

Rather than stop, I kept going and found myself very quickly on the outskirts of Pontevedra. In keeping with my rule, I followed a deviation along a pleasantly wooded riverbank path. The guidebook said this would add just one kilometre to the walk though it seemed a lot longer. But the route was dappled in sunshine and mercifully flat, so I ambled easily into Pontevedra, quite pleased with my progress.

I checked into the Parador – an impressive building set around the core of a renaissance palace – and launched into my usual ablutions and post-walk rituals. I hadn't yet adopted the practice recommended by Carolyn and Laurie of lying on the floor with legs up the wall, but I was sure it was only a matter of time until I did so.

When I met for lunch on the terrace with Toronto's answer to Thelma and Louise, we celebrated my forthcoming promotion to grandfatherhood. My elder daughter, Maeve, had just informed me of her successful first trimester scan, so her hitherto secret pregnancy could now be publicly announced. Always a leader in life's experiences, Laurie already had seven grandchildren and highly recommended the whole business. I was certainly looking forward to it and to everything this new chapter in my life might bring.

Maeve's pregnancy was happy news indeed, but of course it had a poignant edge. Because of her prognosis, Frances knew she was unlikely to live long enough to see any grandchildren. It was something that had been on her mind, as I discovered after my return to England. For the first time I read the journals Frances had kept during what she called her 'bonus years' following her diagnosis. Within them were a number of poems she had written, including one addressed to her potential grandchildren. It was wistful, regretful and full of pathos. It broke my heart.

Little Poem To My Grandchildren

Three score years and ten –
That's all I'd need and, by then,
My children may have had children of their own
And I would be a grandma they had known,
Not just a photo or a snatch of film,
But a living, breathing, cuddling human being.

At the moment, however, we were still in celebratory mood. Accepting the waitress's suggestion we all had the day's special – sweet, succulent clams, washed down with a crisp bottle of Albariño. Perhaps Galicia was beginning to redeem itself gastronomically.

After lunch, while Laurie rested, Carolyn and I roamed the town. I was on a mission to find a stationer's, which I quickly did, thanks to vital information supplied by the Parador's receptionist, who went by the surprisingly Teutonic name of Reiner. I selected some stiff, cream notepaper that I felt would suit my poem.

We visited the baroque Santuario de Peregrina chapel which claimed to have a floor plan shaped like a pilgrim's scallop shell. I would take some convincing that it was anything more than a basic oval – and this despite paying a princely euro to climb to the interior gallery in the dome, the better to appreciate the *'viera'* floor plan.

Afterwards we had a couple of beers and a good chat. Carolyn is a delightful, open soul, full of direct questions that varied from light-hearted topics such as 'what is your favourite Van Morrison song?' to more deeply personal probing. Before becoming a teacher she had worked with her father in the family funeral parlour business, an experience that had furnished her with a wealth of startling stories. I found her company engaging – she was the Canadian equivalent of one of my kindly, good-humoured and, occasionally, earnest American cousins.

In the evening, the three of us shared an adequate but unexciting Parador dinner; our lunchtime clams doomed, it seemed, to remain an all-too-brief culinary high spot.

Wednesday 19 July

Pontevedra to Caldas de Reis

This time it was Laurie's blisters that were causing problems, so the Canadians opted to forgo breakfast in favour of an early start. As usual, I was determined to extract maximum value from the lavish Parador spread, so I set off somewhat later at 9:15. Unfortunately the weather had decided to show its true Galician colours: rain was pouring down into what looked to me to be a grey, spongy Donegal day.

For the first time I donned the cheap and barely adequate rain jacket I had brought along and wrapped my rucksack in its rain cover. I hadn't packed any waterproof trousers so had no choice but to stay in shorts. There was nothing for it but to head across the river and into the sponge.

I resolved simply to walk and try to ignore the rain, but the design of the local houses made that impossible. Rooflines projected well beyond the walls but were devoid of guttering, so cascades of water simply poured on to the pavement. Water thrown up by passing cars didn't help much either. It was pretty miserable going.

By the end of the first hour I was pleased to have notched up 5.2 km and, despite a sore left foot, I felt good about my walking. Just as the rain began to ease I reached a café and was glad to remove my dripping outer jacket. It had failed to keep the moisture off my shirt, which was sodden, as were my shorts thanks to the run-off from the jacket. I sat outside under an awning but quickly realised I was getting chilled in the wind – it was the first time I had actually felt cold on the Camino. I moved indoors and changed into a sporty, long-sleeved Under Armour top in a little games room at the back of the café. That helped immensely but my shorts were still soaked through. My feet, however, felt surprisingly okay.

I was joined at the next table by two pleasant young women from Cologne. One had visited Ireland and talked enthusiastically about Kerry and Bantry Bay in particular. Here was another German who clearly shared Simone's liking for my native land. She was an astonishing example of Teutonic womanhood – tall, statuesque, open-faced and smiling. There was a remarkable but elegant sturdiness to everything about her. She bent her long legs effortlessly, one foot up on the knee of the other, and proceeded to change her socks. Both feet were unblemished – not a blister in sight.

Here was a Rhine maiden, a graceful Valkyrie, to warm Wagner's heart. This young woman was, quite simply, one of the most perfect examples of humanity I had ever seen. I was utterly captivated by her.

These days it is generally frowned upon to pursue such topics, but the Camino throws up distinct examples of the attributes of peoples and nations. Pilgrims are a self-selecting cohort, of course – only the old and the young walk the Camino; the rest of humanity is involved in the tiresome process of 'making a living'. Among the pilgrims I had encountered, Germans were represented in numbers at both ends of the age spectrum, their young noticeable by their sheer physical presence. I had found them among the more earnest but open and pleasant people on the trail. On the debit side, however, they had – the males at least – a fearsome reputation among their fellow hostel users for stentorian snoring. Luckily, given my aversion to such establishments, this was not something I was ever likely to encounter.

Unsurprisingly, there were lots of Spaniards and Portuguese who exuded a cheerful and slightly disorganised air.

As I had discussed with Carolyn and Laurie, many Iberians are strong-featured rather than conventionally handsome people, with a chiselled, sharp-edged look that applies to both men and women. As if to prove the point, in the parish church of Caldas de Reis later that day, I came across a portrait of a particularly masculine-looking nun – a woman predestined perhaps, in those times, to solitary sainthood by her homely looks.

As for pilgrims from nearer home, so far I had encountered not a single English pilgrim nor, somewhat to my surprise, any of my fellow countrymen or women.

In recent years, a series of scandals – shocking even to the most obedient believers – had knocked the Catholic Church off its self-righteous pedestal in Ireland and elsewhere. And, while I understood many Irish people still walked the *Camino Francés*, was it too much to hope that, in the wake of these revelations, the children of Mother Ireland might finally have begun to shake off the rosary-rubbing rigmaroles that had so bedevilled my childhood?

Throughout my boyhood my tribe of Irish were noted for their fervent devotion to all things Catholic. We hadn't gained the accolade of 'isle of saints and scholars' without embracing the full panoply of hair shirts, scapulars and red, raw knees. In the vale of tears that was the material world, penance and self-denial sat easily with the Irish. There was nothing my granny enjoyed more than a grim weekend of prayer and fasting, hobbling barefoot round St Patrick's Purgatory, a bleak penitential island in Lough Derg in Donegal. The Alcatraz of incense it may have been, but, for families like mine, it was a spiritual Butlins camp.

Once, as a boy, I accompanied an uncle to collect granny at the end of one of her regular retreats on the island. As the little ferryboat carrying them back to the mainland came alongside, some of the passengers were still softly muttering prayers. They stepped off with a blissed-out look on their faces, an outer sign of their radiant inner confidence in the indulgences and heavenly rewards their few days of self-denial had secured.

Lough Derg pilgrims spent their first night in wakeful prayer, flitting between the island's church and stumbling in circles round the stations of the cross in the darkness outside. They subsisted on black tea and dry toast for the duration of their stay; their resulting state of grace brought about perhaps as much by sleep deprivation and hunger as spiritual rigour.

And if Lough Derg wasn't enough, the Reek – the sacred mountain of Croagh Patrick on the shores of Clew Bay in county Mayo – provided another honeypot for Ireland's faithful. Every year, thousands of prayer-mumbling devotees climbed its 764 metres – many in bare feet; some on their knees – to the greater honour and glory of our patron saint.

What is it about pilgrims and bare feet? In his quirky and entertaining book *'Byways, Boots and Blisters: A History of Walkers and Walking'*, Bill Laws mentions the Slipper Chapel which lay a mile from the shrine of Our Lady of Walsingham in Norfolk, a destination which competed with Canterbury as the prime object of ambulant devotion in medieval England.

On arrival at the Slipper Chapel, pilgrims removed their footwear before walking the final stretch to the shrine barefoot. Henry VIII did so in 1511, becoming the last King of England to undertake this particular penance. Of course, Henry made it impossible for any successor to follow in his footsteps – 27 years after his visit, during the dissolution of the monasteries, he had Walsingham's venerated image of the Virgin brought to London and burned.

I was pleased to note that none of my fellow pilgrims showed any of these extremes of barefoot devotion. All were more than adequately shod, so the shareholders of Salomon, Merrell, Berghaus etc could rest easy in their beds. And, to judge by the ambling, lazy shuffle that many of my walking companions adopted despite their sporting footwear, few were in any rush to encounter St James.

The slack-legged pilgrim shuffle was something I simply could not emulate. It was just one of many Camino walking styles, but by far the most popular. There were young people who walked like ancients, and elders who seemed to glide effortlessly along. There were scruffs and ragamuffins of all sorts, but also incredibly tidy, organised souls with every bit of kit neatly clipped in its proper place. Others were wandering washing lines, drying laundry pegged to their rucksacks, gussets dancing in the breeze.

Occasionally I overtook groups of youngsters, led by priests or teachers, all invariably clad in identical hats or t-shirts. Other bands of more free-spirited young people strolled along, singing and joking and clearly, like me, picking up most of their *Credencial* stamps in bars and bordellos along the way – well, perhaps, not so many of the latter in my case.

I had no idea what sort of picture I presented as I strode along – perhaps that of a demented Orangeman who had started marching on 12 July and simply carried on. I knew one thing: no one walked faster on the Camino. I was constantly overtaking people but only cyclists overtook me. I was not being competitive: I just enjoyed the rhythm of stretching my legs and walking at pace. Sometimes, however, I had to remind myself to slow down, to take time to savour my surroundings – to stay in the moment. But overall, I was delighted at my stamina. Even the longer, hotter days, I felt, took little out of me. Indeed, at one point on the previous day, about 12 kilometres out of Pontevedra, I suddenly found a second wind and simply upped my pace. Another time, however, I had consciously to attempt to stop stomping on my heels and adopt a more rolling gait in an effort to spread the load more evenly over my soles and so minimise damage to my feet.

I soon reached my next stop: the bar Cuberto, just a few kilometres outside Caldas de Reis, my final destination for the day. A functional barn of a place, the Cuberto was ruled by an affable, multi-lingual host who, as each customer entered, demanded to know their nationality. Once informed, he delighted himself by launching into a welcoming exchange in his guests' native tongue. I downed a refreshing 1906 and, as the sun had finally come out, was content to move on without lunch and soon reached Caldas.

While I was at the Cuberto, Carolyn contacted me to let me know she and Laurie were staying at the Acuña hotel and asked if I wanted them to get me a room. They had also booked massages: was I interested? The Balneario Acuña was a spa hotel: Caldas, it appeared, was renowned for its health-giving hot springs. I was dubious about the massage but jumped at the offer of a room. I could then just bimble into town, secure in the knowledge I had a bed for the night.

The Acuña turned out to be a lovely, old-style establishment with the slightly dowdy, frayed around the edges feel that I like in hotels of a certain age. I was set up with a fine room on the third floor with separate balconies off my bedroom and bathroom, both overlooking the river.

I had completed almost 20 km in about five hours, with two stops, and felt good about it. So much so that, for the first time, I even tried the Canadian recovery position: lying on the bathroom floor with my feet up the wall. It was a tough position to get into but no doubt in some immeasurable way beneficial. Clearly, staying in a *balneario* might be having an effect.

A notice in my room outlining the proper use of towels contained the finest example of Spanglish I had encountered so far: 'If it leaves to the towel in the bathtub or the shower, we will change it. If it leaves in hung in the towel rack we understand that it wishes to use it once again'. I suspected Google Translate bore some responsibility for the production of such gobbledegook. Googledegook perhaps?

After besmirching at least one balcony with dripping sportswear, I set out into the town. I wanted to visit the parochial church which, to my surprise, was dedicated to the martyred English (or, perhaps more correctly, Norman) Archbishop of Canterbury, Thomas à Beckett. I was indulging in some tenuous connection with it as a result of Frances's funeral having been held in the similarly dedicated church of Thomas à Beckett near our home in Portsmouth.

A pleasant town with much dignified domestic architecture, Caldas de Reis clearly made good use of the hot springs that gave it its name. The waters had been flowing at a constant temperature for centuries and still attracted thousands of visitors annually. Hobbling pilgrims were well catered for, as a couple of giggling Camino girls had discovered as they lay stretched out in the street, soothing their feet in a trough of warm water spilling from two spouting lions' mouths.

After a couple of 1906s in a dreary bar I headed back to the hotel with a mixture of anticipation and dread. Against my better judgment, I had booked an upper body massage – quite a departure from my usual quinine-based pre-dinner regime.

Massage was just one of various fleshly indulgences offered by the hotel. These ranged from Deep Sea Mud Therapy to 'Color Peeling – corporal exfoliation using essential salts and oils to regenerate the epidermis'. My *parcial massage* – the only option available by the time I made my booking – promised a relaxing massage of the upper body 'from the cervical to gluteus'. I couldn't wait to discover if I possessed either of those things.

Ignorant of massage etiquette, I decided it was probably best to wear my swimming trunks. Despite my beer-infused pilgrim regime, these were now surprisingly loose and threatened to embrace my ankles at any moment. Then, suitably wrapped in one of the pristine white robes supplied with my room, I descended to the basement and prepared to lose my massage virginity.

A smiling young woman instructed me to take a seat while she slipped into a room to tell the previous client his time was up. Out he came, wearing an identical hotel robe and carrying what I assumed to be his shorts. I didn't quite pick up on this visual signal before I was invited into the room and told to stretch myself along the massage table.

As the lights dimmed and lugubrious music started up, the masseuse departed. Discarding my robe but keeping my swimming trunks on, I lay face down, looking through the hole at the head of the table. Moments later, without my realising she was back, the masseuse was at my side, silently raising the table to work height. Immediately she started tugging at the waistband of my trunks but, as my body weight was on them, they didn't yield much. In some confusion, I couldn't decide if I should raise my front to facilitate whatever she was trying to achieve.

When she covered my arse end with a small towel that had been lying in the middle of the table when I arrived, I realised I had made whatever the Spanish is for *faux pas*: I should have been naked. But it was too late. Hopping up and ripping off my trunks at this point would probably not have been a good idea. I lay there, rigid with embarrassment and with the rueful realisation that, whatever the gluteus aspect of the procedure involved, residual Irish Catholic modesty had ensured I was going to be denied it.

The ritual started with cool oil or unguent being poured along my spine from neck to buttock-defending waistband. Then the masseuse worked it all over and began kneading my back, sides, shoulders and neck. This went on for a long time and, despite the gongs and twangs of the inevitable whale music groaning in the background, it was pleasant and relaxing. Eventually the table was lowered and I was told I had five minutes to relax and chill. Needless to say I couldn't sustain relaxation for that length of time and was soon back in my room, showering off the remnants of the sacred oils.

After my self-sacrifice on the altar of bodily worship, it was time for more normal preprandial pursuits. I found a large subterranean bar where I seemed to be the only customer. The friendly Spanish barmaid poured me a generous G&T and then asked: 'Where's that accent from? Is it Ballymena or Derry?'

I was astonished – mostly at the suggestion that I sounded like I came from a God-forsaken place like Ballymena. Or perhaps she had mistaken me for Liam Neeson, a proud native of those parts.

The barmaid explained that her husband was from Belfast and they had lived in Northern Ireland for many years. She had sampled the delights of the province and even claimed to know my home town. After the birth of their son, they had moved to Spain because she wanted him brought up Spanish among her family who hailed from an island off the coast of Galicia. Her son was called Jamie – the only Jamie in these parts she assured me – and spoke Spanish with a Northern Irish accent. Her husband was teaching English locally – in a Belfast accent, I hoped – and she greatly regretted that he wasn't around to meet a fellow countryman.

After this enjoyable encounter I adjourned to the hotel terrace where I kept a watchful eye on a volatile sky. It might have been coincidence but, a few minutes after I sat down, the music playing through the outdoor speakers switched to Van Morrison. A sweet gesture, if it was the barmaid's.

With both the sky and my stomach rumbling, I didn't hang about to see if I would be treated to Sir Van's entire oeuvre. I went indoors and joined Carolyn and Laurie in the noisy dining room which seemed to be populated by a fair percentage of the geriatrics of Galicia.

My companions were not in the best of moods. Despite being seated on the river side of the room, they complained that they couldn't see the water. Sightlines from the table were obstructed by a thick, horizontal glazing bar. This formed part of a gallery structure that rose three storeys high, covering almost the entire north side of the building. From the outside, it gave the hotel a light and airy look and reminded me of the tall, galleried houses we had seen on our 1994 trip in La Corunna on Galicia's north coast. Nothing could be done about our architectural blindspot, so I just hoped something temptingly visual might soon arrive on a plate to distract us.

It was not to be. Carolyn and Laurie's prebooked tour clearly included the Pilgrim's menu as their prepaid dinner choice each evening. A common feature in hotels and restaurants along the Camino, these menus had furnished many of my good value lunches en route, but it was a hit and miss option. I joined them in opting for the pilgrim's fare but it delivered such a lacklustre meal that Carolyn resolved never again to eat anything with the word 'pilgrim' attached to it. Based on that evening's experience, I could only concur.

After dinner we crossed the road to what appeared to be a very rundown or even defunct taverna. But, once we worked our way through to the riverside, it turned out to be a busy, lively place. A line of chill cabinets, filled with tempting cuts of well-hung meat, rubbed salt in our recent gastric injuries. Why hadn't we known about this place? We could have had a much better dinner here.

Laurie was in the mood for an after-dinner drink and mentioned a yen for a glass of Port. I explained there was no chance of finding Port where we were. In the surprisingly parochial world of European regional drinking, no Galician barman would think of stocking Port, even though Porto was only a handful of kilometres to the south. Defeated, she toyed with the possibility of sweet sherry as an alternative. We discussed Pedro Ximenez but, again, I cautioned that, despite being Spanish, it was unlikely to be available so far from its Andalusian base.

We consulted our waiter and, after much pooh-poohing of both Port and sweet sherry as options, he dived into a corner of the bar and produced with a flourish a bottle of Osborne Fino – the driest of sherries. But he was so pleased with himself that none of us could decline. Laurie sucked up her dry after-dinner aperitif in a non-complaining way that could only do credit to her native land. By way of reward, just before we were about to leave, the waiter returned with slices of beautifully light sponge cake – on the house.

In its ramshackle way the taverna had been one of the best places I'd encountered so far. If I ever found myself back in Caldas, I would head straight there. And, like many previously wonderful places discovered while travelling, it would probably have gone downhill or even shut up shop. Such is the way.

Needless to say, Carolyn left a magnificent tip. These Canadians were serious tippers, clearly competing in open-handedness with their cousins south of the 49th parallel. They told me they left €5 each per night for the chambermaids in their hotels, making my small contributions of a few Euros appear very miserly.

On one of our previous rambles, Carolyn had handed over a €5 note to pay a beer tab of €3.40 – a 50 per cent tip, as I pointed out. I tried to explain that European tipping culture was more of a rounding up process, but Carolyn was having none of it. Hers was a generous soul and those who served her well along the way would know the benefit.

Thursday 20 July

Caldas de Reis to Padrón

My eleventh day on the road. Maybe the stages were getting less demanding or my body was finally fitter but, for whatever reason, the walk from Caldas to Padrón proved to be the easiest of my Camino so far. Of course, much of it was down to the fact that I was finally walking in comfort – not exactly blister-free but the worst of the blisters had burst, reduced or hardened and so were not causing any pain.

As usual, Carolyn and Laurie had set out earlier but I stayed for breakfast at the hotel – a decision that led to another new resolution for my future travelling plans. I determined to give up on breakfasts in hotels – or at least the buffet-style variety – now, alas, an almost universal format. The whole process involved far too much work, with too many choices, too much fiddly equipment and multiple opportunities for stress and confusion at the beginning of one's day.

That morning I failed to extract so much as a dribble from a baffling orange juice container. Like one of those wretched coffee jugs that can also throw me into an early morning panic, the juice jalopy sported a proliferation of knobs, levers and buttons with no clear indication of their functions. I applied myself to all but the large knob on top which, it turned out, was the one that actually squirted the juice. I learned this when a fellow guest (hailing, I had no doubt, from somewhere close to Samaria), noting my incompetence, came across to show me how it was done.

I live for the day when a benign and omnipotent world government decrees there will be only one style of coffee jug and one model of slowly cranking, inefficient conveyor belt toaster in all the hotels on the planet.

It had not been a good start and, by the time I had trolled back and forth from my table to the buffet area, made my coffee, cut my bread, searched to see where the butter had been hidden, then returned for honey, fruit etc, I decided I had waited on myself so assiduously I owed myself a tip. And I had probably walked a distance equivalent to at least half of that day's Camino stage.

So, I was done with buffet breakfasts. I had already sampled the option of a 'tostada after the first few kilometres, as practised by the Canadians, and I knew it suited me. But, on the bright side, I was so distracted by the hard labour of serving myself that I failed to notice what, if any, piped music was playing.

I caught up with Carolyn and Laurie at another of their traditional layovers: the 11:00 am Coke stop – for the drink, that is, which Laurie needed for her blood sugar, not the powdery stuff. Afterwards we walked on together. We had made good time so I didn't feel any need to rush. It was a relatively short stage – 19 km – so we would reach Padrón quite quickly. I telephoned the Pension Jardin, where my friends had a room reserved, and secured a bed for the night.

Padrón turned out to be another pleasant, unpretentious town. We strolled in along the river Sar, took in the market, which was winding to a close, and stopped for a beer in an impressive *paseo* space shaded by plane trees.

As we wandered through the quiet streets I spotted a small restaurant, A Casa dos Martínez, which boasted a Michelin Guide recommendation. I've always been a bit of a sucker for Michelin-approved eateries: perhaps this one had also been awarded a few tyres? As we stood outside, the reassuringly rotund chef came out to tempt us with his menu. This was accompanied by a red file containing large colour photographs of his typical dishes. Normally I would run a mile from restaurants that displayed photographs of their food but it was clear this was our kindly chef's way of reassuring and educating gastronomically timid foreigners.

The menu certainly looked promising but, the chef explained, as he worked on the principle of market availability on the day – always a good thing in my view – he wouldn't know until later what he would actually be offering. Happily seduced despite (or because of) this proviso, we signed up for dinner at 8:00.

Pension Jardin turned out to be a splendid old building, crammed with typically heavy Spanish furniture on steroids – the sort that would give an average removal man a massive hernia. And, despite the addition of pilgrim-proof plastic covering the stair carpet, the place had the old world charm of a comfortably aged colonial home.

We lunched in a nearby restaurant and then, while Laurie rested, Carolyn and I set out on our, by now, customary sightseeing ramble. Unfortunately, due to my misreading the map, we had great difficulty establishing the whereabouts of the *Casa* Museum of a famed local poet, Rosalia de Castro – a producer of 'lugubrious verse', according to my guidebook. We reached the edge of town before realising the *Casa* lay much further on, so we decided to give it a miss and spared ourselves any risk of contagion from *Señora* Castro's sorrowful ballads.

On the way back, I addressed my complaints about the general blandness of the town's eponymous peppers to a fine bronze statue of a doleful *pementeira* – a female pepper seller who was doing very little business on her plinth on a traffic island. She offered me very little explanation either.

We moved on to the church of Santiago which contains the original mooring stone that gave Padrón its name. The legend has it that, in the days before the town's harbour silted up, the boat carrying the body of the martyred St James tied up to this stone on its arrival in Galicia. An illustration of the event formed the centrepiece of the fine *Credencial* stamp we obtained from an enthusiastic sacristan at the church. It was easily the most artistic stamp I had collected thus far and, for once, of impeccable ecclesiastical pedigree.

When Laurie rejoined us just before dinner, we returned to the bar in the plane tree *paseo*. In the space outside a number of men were playing a boules-like game. It involved flinging small balls at a metal arrow, leading to much clanging and banging and ribald exchanges among the participants.

Undaunted by the previous evening's sherry fiasco, Laurie was continuing her quest for a European aperitif: this time the target liquid was Campari. Once again she drew a blank, but our hostess held out the promise of a '100% Pedro Ximenez' option. After much shuffling through dusty bottles under the bar, this turned out to be a pale PX from Montilla-Moriles, not its dark, prune-like Jerez equivalent. And again, alas, not quite what Laurie had been seeking.

But our rotund Michelin man did not disappoint – though he astonished us by serving up ice-chilled red Rioja and Ribero del Duero. Carolyn chose seafood salad while Laurie had prawns and guacamole. Given her Mexican residency, she had been missing bashed up avocados.

I opted for pork cheeks – 'like my grandmother' the menu informed me – presumably 'used to make', I trusted. The cheeks had been cooking for five hours, the chef assured me, and they were certainly tender and fell apart easily. But, yet again, the dish lacked flavour – the accompanying sauce would have benefited mightily from a bit more unctuous intensity. Where was our good friend Pedro Ximenez when we needed him?

We shared a tomato salad that consisted of huge red chunks of flesh that looked more like watermelon. It was delicious. All in all, it was an honest, simple meal but the best of the Camino so far – a judgment Laurie duly communicated to our host. Clearly delighted, he asked if he could take our photograph for his Facebook page and, within minutes, Carolyn was able to show me we were indeed up there as *'Peregrinos Gastronomicos'* – and also, for some unfathomable reason, as fans of the TV series 'Game of Thrones'!

Such Facebook agility – if not veracity – was further ammunition for Carolyn's increasingly intense campaign to get me to sign up with the dreaded social network. Back at the *pension* she treated me to a teacherly tutorial on how items were posted and what she shared with her 421 friends. Much to her disgust, her brother, a musician, numbered his 'friends' in the thousands.

I was touched by her kindness but made it clear that signing up with Facebook would be the last thing I would consider. Both Canadians, however, confidently predicted that, as soon as my grandchild arrived, I would be up there, keen to share every meaningful smile and dental eruption with a grateful online audience.

Friday 21 July

Padrón to Teo

As usual, my fellow travellers set off early. Carolyn and Laurie had 25 km to complete in order to reach Santiago. I was breaking my journey and so faced a mere 11 km to a *Casa Rural* called Paradas de Francos. This had been highly recommended to me by a woman I met back home while planning my hike. She had just returned from a week walking the final stages of the *Camino Portugués* and said the Paradas had been the most relaxing and idyllic place she had stayed in. It was also ideally situated to ensure an easy amble into Santiago on the last day, in time for the midday pilgrims' Mass.

So I cancelled my original booking for the Hotel Moure in Santiago for Friday 21st – the very hotel, as it turned out, in which Carolyn and Laurie were spending the last two nights of their trip. The *Casa Rural* was accepting only two-night reservations but, as I thought I might welcome a break before the end of my hike, I was happy to acquiesce. I then booked a room in the Hostal dos Reis Católicos, Santiago's renowned five-star Parador, for the night of my arrival in the city. All seemed sorted for a chilled and indulgent ending to my Camino.

As I walked through Padrón to pick up the trail, I met our portly chef from the previous evening. He was a man in a hurry, anxious perhaps to bank his takings from the night before or heading to the market to replenish his store of grandma's cheeks. He greeted me warmly, as we 'Game of Thrones' fans do, and we parted the best of friends.

But I couldn't help worrying about the longevity of his business. He had had only four customers while we were there – the sainted trinity of gastronomic pilgrims and a quiet Belgian who dragged himself reluctantly away before curfew at his pilgrim hostel. Here was a man in no hurry to experience the delights of such an establishment for the first time.

The walk was much like the previous day – easy and gentle but with a few sections along the dreaded N550, a road I had come to detest as the Camino had switched back and forth, across and along it at multiple points since Porto.

Suddenly – and astonishingly swiftly, it seemed – I reached my destination. Set in a quiet hamlet, the Parada de Francos soon revealed itself to be not the most welcoming of hostelries. I have a particular detestation of bossy notices aimed at guests in public establishments – the sort designed to make the *hoi polloi* mind their Ps and Qs – and the Parada quickly proved itself to be one of the worst offenders I had ever encountered.

In my bedroom, a notice listed the cost of the quality items so generously supplied for my comfort: 'We remember the prices of the products that intend to provide a good stay in this hotel' as the English translation helpfully explained. Once again, it seemed, Google Translate had opened up yawning canyons of linguistic hazard for its users.

The comprehensive list extended from quilt, cushions and keys to bed sheets, pillows and hair dryer, all with, I was sure, inflated prices. The cost of replacing the hair dryer was €120 (oh yeah!) while the towels were a snip at a mere €30 each. Furthermore and verbatim: 'ANY FAULT OR DESPERFECT OF THE SAME WILL BE CHARGED IN THE CARD AS WELL AS THE WASTE'. All of this, of course, was written in capitals, so obviously intended to be read VERY LOUDLY.

An accompanying notice outlined 'RULES OF GOOD CONDUCT', reminding me, when in the common room or lounge, not to put my feet on the couch. Also: 'YOU CAN

NOT WALK BAREFOOT THROUGH THE RESTAURANT' and 'PLEASE DO NOT YELL THERE ARE MORE PEOPLE IN THE HOTEL AND MAY BE SLEEPING'. A further notice on the terrace forbade bringing food on to the premises because 'WE SELL FOOD'.

But the final straw came when I discovered the bar stocked not a single Galician beer. The only brew was Mahou from Madrid, another of Spain's dreaded generic *amarillo* lagers. I upbraided the owner for stocking a beer from the centre of the country rather than a fine regional tipple like 1906. To be fair, he seemed to take this in good part but, after my departure, a notice would no doubt be going up warning that 'RECOGNITION CONSIDERATIONS ON BEER SERVED IN PROMISES WILL NOT BE TOLERATED'.

I quickly made my mind up about one thing: I did not want to spend the whole of the following day in this hellhole. I tried to persuade the owner to let me cancel my second night, but that was a route he wasn't prepared to pioneer, even if I threatened to plant my dusty pilgrim footwear on his precious couch. I had already paid upfront on my credit card so I resolved to take the hit and look for somewhere in Santiago for the following evening.

I choked down a couple of cold Mahou (which at least was slightly more tolerable than the equally ubiquitous

Cruzcampo) and followed up with a substantial lunch of prawn and mushroom omelette. My requested tomato salad arrived as a standard Spanish mixed salad, complete with hard-boiled egg, white asparagus and chunks of tuna. I passed the rest of the afternoon usefully, transcribing copies of my 'Frances Farewell' poem on to the notepaper I had bought in Pontevedra.

Eventually dinnertime rolled round and, just as at lunch, I was the sole diner. The place was a morgue. I would go mad if I had to stay another day – but at least I could read the notices as loudly as I liked that night. It was clear no one else 'MAY BE SLEEPING'. I paid for my meals and drinks and told the owner I would be moving on in the morning. Raising his eyes briefly from the television in the bar, he rewarded me with the slightest of shrugs.

With the feast of St James – its biggest celebration of the year – just a few days away, Santiago was filling up. After some difficulty, I managed to secure a room in a modest *pension* not far from the centre. This meant that I wasn't going to enjoy the classic Camino finish I had intended: arriving, a road-weary pilgrim, into the great cathedral square before being assumed immediately into the majesty of the 15th century Hostal dos Reís Católicos. No matter: any place would be better than the hell of NOTICEBOARD CENTRAL.

Saturday 22 July

Teo to Santiago de Compostela

My last day on the Camino and, beyond my bedroom window, the prospect was certainly grey. Exhausting the final choices of my sporting clobber, I selected the long-sleeved Under Armour top for only its second outing, thinking this would deal with any unseasonal low temperatures. But, just as I stepped out the door, it started to rain. I nipped back in, dug out my outer jacket and the cover for my rucksack and prepared for a watery final stage. As a result, it was just after half past seven when I set off into a dull, dreich day.

Despite the rain, the walking was easy, with long but relatively gentle climbs. It was a case of just plodding on, dripping from every surface. As I approached Milladorio,

Santiago's allegedly upmarket but truly hideous new suburb, the rain began to ease. Dropping from there, the towers of the great cathedral became visible for the first time. The end was in sight.

Unfortunately, as I drew nearer Santiago, I lost the yellow Camino arrows at one point and, as a result, clearly picked the wrong option at a confusing junction. The main road had a broad pavement, however, so I decided to follow it in the general direction of the city. But, after a few hundred metres, the pavement ended, just as I arrived at a complicated roundabout fed by a series of slip roads, some leading on and off what appeared to be a motorway.

I was concerned I might end up wandering on to the motorway by mistake but, somehow, managed to negotiate my way safely across the junctions. It was Saturday morning, so traffic was light and I soon found myself back on my old enemy, the N550. Gritting my teeth, I resolved to follow it into the city.

This time the N550 redeemed itself by quickly hooking up with the Way and I soon had a plethora of yellow arrows to guide me up the long climb to the historic centre. Crossing through a park, I found my way on to the *Rúa do Franco*, the traditional entry route to the city centre for pilgrims arriving from the *Camino Portugués*.

Back in 1994, when I first visited Santiago, the Camino was in a sorry state. Many sections had fallen into disuse and accommodation options along the route were much more limited. Pilgrims had a tougher time of it then, so the arrival in Santiago was an emotional high point after what had perhaps been a true ordeal. I had watched bearded, tousle-headed pilgrims fall to their knees sobbing in front of the cathedral. Now, arrival was a more triumphal affair, with flags and music and groups striding into the square, whooping and singing what was presumably their adopted anthem of the Way.

Standing in the great square of the Obradoiro in front of the cathedral, I felt surprisingly little emotion at completing my own Camino, but I was happy to be back in Santiago and keen to see how much the city had changed now it had again become a major global destination.

I had walked about 220 kilometres and had enjoyed the experience immensely. As someone who had never previously hiked two days in succession, I felt a genuine sense of achievement. I had relished moments of solitude and contemplation along the way, but also enjoyed glancing encounters with fellow travellers. I had suffered no real hardships – other than the inevitable blisters and the occasional substandard beer. Above all, I had been warmly embraced by Carolyn and Laurie, whose kindness and good company had brightened my pathway immensely. But, as for spiritual growth and the other intangible or inward aspects of the Camino that resonated with so many of my fellow travellers, as a mere pond skater on the meniscus of life, I knew I was incapable of such insights.

Just as our voluble Pousada prattler back in Valença had warned, the great west front of the cathedral was wrapped in scaffolding and the entrance barred. As a result, there was no access to the celebrated *Pórtico da Gloria*, the ornate main doorway into the church and the sculptural masterpiece of Master Mateo, builder of the cathedral. Indeed the whole square was a bit of a building site. Facing the cathedral, the magnificent neoclassical Pazo de Raxoi, the seat of local government, appeared to be completely closed for a major refurbishment. Two large cranes stood in front of it and the area was sealed off by tape. This was by no means the spiritually uplifting conclusion of the road to glory that many of my fellow travellers might have hoped for.

Feeling decidedly sodden and a bit low key myself, I opted to collect my *Compostela* before visiting the cathedral. Carolyn had warned me about the horrendous wait 'on line' that she and Laurie had endured the previous day, so I headed down some steps past the Parador and turned right to the Camino office. A motley crew of pilgrims was waiting patiently but we weren't too numerous and, by good luck, after a mere ten minutes I was called through to what was a modern, busy, multilingual office. The moment had come to put the final seal on my *Credencial*.

I was directed to a seat in front of a desk occupied by a kind-faced, mature woman (truth be told, she may well have been younger than me). I handed over my *Credencial*, its 33 stamps a record of my progress through the watering holes and fleshpots along the way. Taking her time, my assessor studied it carefully, no doubt inwardly tut-tutting at the number of licensed premises rather than godly outposts that featured in it. Finally, carefully folding it up, she looked directly at me and asked: 'And why did you do the Camino, Patrick?'

To my utter astonishment, I found myself choking, then sobbing and finally bursting into tears as I replied: 'I did the Camino to say goodbye to my wife who died last year'.

Clearly moved, the good woman shot round from her side of the desk, wrapped her arms round me in a tight hug and muttered some comforting words. One of her colleagues at another desk reached across and held my hands.

Once I'd stopped sobbing I explained that, when I started out, I hadn't known that was the reason I had decided to walk the Camino but it had quickly become clear to me in the course of the walk. The woman said my wife would always be with me and I said I felt she had done the Camino alongside me. It had been an extraordinary moment and, perhaps, in some way confirmed that there had, after all, been some sort of 'spiritual' element to my hike.

As a result of my fine show of emotion, the kind lady informed me that, not only would I receive the official Camino stamp to mark the end of my pilgrimage, but she was also awarding me an additional, special stamp – an illustration of the tomb of the apostle itself. Both were duly pressed with fitting ceremony on to the final sheet of my *Credencial*.

After mulling over the Latin spelling of Patrick in the accusative case for my *Compostela* – which proved to be a colourful A4 sheet in the style of a medieval illuminated manuscript – she settled on *Patricium*, with which I concurred. I just managed to hold myself back from pointing out that, as my surname in Gaelic means 'grandson of a lord', perhaps we could consider some declension of *nepos domini* to complete my Latinate conversion. It had, I thought, a fine ecclesiastical ring, but my scribe settled simply for the bald, anglicised Tierney.

Then I was asked where I had set out from to start my Camino. We had already established that, though I was Irish, I lived in Britain, so I said I had arrived from England. It was explained that an announcement at the Pilgrims' Mass at noon would mention a pilgrim starting from Porto. Did I want this to be an English or Irish pilgrim? Well, obviously, it had to be *Irlandés*.

Finally, after the tiniest of hesitations, I filled in a form stating that the purpose of my Camino had been 'spiritual' rather than 'religious'. I received my *Compostela* with due ceremony and was free to go.

There was just time to find my *Pension* and have a shower before the Pilgrims' Mass at noon which, despite my atheism, I was determined to attend. I was hoping the *botafumeiro* might be in action. This is a massive thurible which is swung to roof height across the transept of the cathedral by a team of eight men. For centuries it had been used to waft incense through the cathedral, possibly to defeat the stench caused by massed ranks of putrid pilgrims.

At the *Pension* I had to choose between a large room on the fourth floor or what turned out to be little more than a broom cupboard on the first. But, with no lift and as I was carrying my full kit, the near lightless monk's cell on the first floor was the clear winner. For one night, who cared?

I hadn't made it into the shower before Carolyn messaged to say she was holding a seat for me in the rapidly filling cathedral, but wasn't sure how much longer she could do so. Even though it was only 11:00, she suggested getting over there quickly. I decided to forgo my ablutions and just hoped the *botafumeiro* would be up to the task of masking my Camino aroma. Despite my saltiness, Carolyn was mightily relieved when I joined her in the pew, as did Laurie shortly after.

It was a long wait for showtime. Bells rang, lights came on, an increasingly exasperated official prowled the rows near us, unsuccessfully demanding that we be quiet. A nun with a beautiful soprano voice and very clear hand indications of rising and falling notes – obviously an experienced choir mistress – patiently took the whole congregation through the sung responses for the Mass. People joined in haphazardly, but the good sister was relentlessly positive and encouraging, though it was clear her amplified voice alone would have been enough to fill the huge space.

A long queue snaked from the left side of the sanctuary, round behind the high altar and then ascended to allow people to touch or hug the statue of St James who stared down at the growing multitude. I remembered doing this in 1994 with Frances and the children. Then there had hardly been any queue. This time, watching parents lift their children up to embrace the statue or help them back down the steps, I found myself getting quite emotional. I was thinking of Frances and me, 23 years previously, in our prime, with our lovely young family. Where had all those years gone?

Finally, after multiple exhortations in Spanish, English, German and French urging us not to take photographs or videos during the 'celebration', a shambling, lackadaisical procession of clerics entered from just behind us. Clearly the clergy were determined to maintain the pilgrim shuffle to the bitter end.

Two bishops, looking very pleased with themselves, followed behind. One was a visiting prelate from Palermo, who had led a large group of pilgrims from Italy. They strolled on into the sanctuary to begin Mass.

But first a lengthy introduction listed the provenance of all the pilgrims who had arrived in the city that day, as well as their points of departure. There were some poor souls from Syria and, of course, a shout-out for 'Irish pilgrim setting out from Porto'. Good for him.

Slowly the ceremony got under way, with the heroic nun leading the singing and also helpfully indicating when we should stand or sit. Very little kneeling was required – even during the consecration – something my arthritic lower limbs appreciated.

The resident bishop gave a lengthy sermon without notes, weaving in Santiago and Mary Magdalene, whose feast day it happened to be. As all the readings had been given in both Spanish and Italian, in honour of our new pals from Palermo, I was terrified the entire sermon would be repeated for their benefit, but we were spared that fate.

My Catholic upbringing involved frequent doses of Gregorian chant on high days and holidays and I still find great delight in liturgical music. At times during the service I found myself moved with what I can only imagine was some tinge of regret for what I had left behind. I agree with the 19th century sociologist Thorstein Veblen that religion is 'the fabrication of vendible imponderables in the nth dimension'. It is, without doubt, the most successful business model ever devised: the expensive insurance policy that is never called upon to deliver.

At the funerals of relatives or friends, I find it infuriating when glib promises of eternal life and all the paradisiacal topdressing that goes with it are droned out in clear English. But, in a foreign tongue, such platitudes somehow sound more acceptable. Intoned in Spanish or Italian, these pious nostrums wash over me like a mellifluous balm. When the *Pater Noster* was sung, I felt particularly moved: it was the first time I had heard the 'Our Father' since Frances's funeral.

Eventually the business concluded, alas without the *botafumeiro* raising a puff of smoke. It seemed it is only used in Holy Years and at the Friday evening Pilgrims' Mass, so Carolyn and Laurie had missed a trick by not attending the previous evening.

After Mass I went back to the *Pension* to shower and change and then met up again with my Canadians for an excellent lunch of clams and octopus on the Rúa da Raíña, a crowded street lined with tempting seafood establishments.

Our chosen venue was opposite my intended eating-place, the San Jamie, a tapas restaurant that had been recommended by a friend at home. But, as the day was bright and sunny, we wanted to dine *al fresco*. In the narrow street the custom was for the restaurants to switch pavement seating between the two sides on alternate days. It seemed a very civilised arrangement, so we opted to forego the potential delights of San Jaime in favour of the sun-kissed tables opposite.

After my earlier spiritual exertions, I needed a lie-down. Carolyn was keen to go sightseeing, while Laurie was in a mood for shopping, so we agreed to go our separate ways until aperitif time.

After a much-needed siesta, I wandered over to the Moure Hotel and hung about outside in what felt like full stalker mode, but Carolyn and Laurie weren't in the least perturbed as they hailed me from an upstairs window. We wandered down the street for drinks in a bright, flower-filled patio attached to another hotel. By this point, a defeated Laurie had given up the hunt for obscure aperitifs and was happy to join us as we settled for gin and tonics.

It was my Canadians last night in Santiago and Laurie announced that she would like pasta for dinner. We headed to Café Casino, a place recommended by their holiday organiser. A huge room, lined with dark wood and interesting and, at times, grotesque bas-relief panels, it had a distinctly touristy air. I feared it might be a repeat of my experience at the Majestic Café in Porto, supplier of one of the stodgiest meals I had ever eaten, but it proved to be a touch more refined. Laurie and I shared a Galician lobster on linguine, accompanied by a very good Albariño.

Suddenly a hunched 'monk' in brown robes hobbled into the centre of the dining room to kick off some weird after-dinner entertainment. Heavily mic-ed up, he proceeded to fling ingredients into a steaming cauldron which he stirred dramatically, all the while loudly chanting spells and incantations. We were clearly witnessing the concoction of the Queimada, allegedly a traditional Celtic punch involving rough spirit, bits of fruit and peel and, rather surprisingly, coffee beans. Blue flames leapt from the cauldron to heighten the drama and ensure the distillation of the potent spiritual powers this hocus pocus druidic pantomime promised. The first sip of Queimada is supposed to banish evil spirits, the second frees the mind of prejudice while the third – should one get that far – promises to ignite passion in the soul!

I thought the whole performance would frighten a couple of children at a nearby table but, instead, it was I who freaked out when Laurie proposed we sample this 'traditional Galician' concoction as a post-prandial liqueur. I wasn't particularly interested in swallowing something I suspected would taste revolting, but, as I had got dinner, Laurie was insisting on buying the liqueurs. Three tiny earthenware cups of this dubious draught were duly supplied. Rather lemony, with all the alcohol clearly burnt off in the theatrical blue flames, it produced no discernible spiritual benefits and had little to recommend it other than reassuring me that the services of the coroner would probably not be required.

After dinner we joined the audience at an outdoor concert in the Praza da Quintana where the steps up to the cathedral acted as a ready-made amphitheatre facing a large stage. A six-piece band called Milladorio – surely they weren't named after the city's hideous suburb? – treated us to lively Galician folk tunes. *Gaitas* – the Galician bagpipes – featured strongly and, to my delight, were joined at times by what could have been either Breton or Irish Uilleann pipes.

Skilled multi-instrumentalists, the band members were totally at ease with one another and clearly enjoying the music as much as their audience. Occasionally a pair of dancers clasped and unclasped as they wheeled and arced across the stage and, at one point, they were joined by a troupe of what I assumed to be visiting Irish dancers. In vivid green costumes they lined up along the front of the platform, leaping and clattering to the delight of all.

The performance reminded me of how instantly appealing and familiar I had found Galician music during our 1994 visit. This time, too, I felt I could have been in Galway or Donegal. This was certainly Celtic music and, while the band was a good deal less polished than outfits like the Chieftains, they were all the more likeable for their rougher, barn dance edge. Needless to say, I bought a CD. It would be interesting to see how it would hold up under the grey skies of England.

After a couple of hours of non-stop music it was time to say goodbye to Carolyn and Laurie. Their companionship, especially on the stopovers, had made my Camino a much more enjoyable experience than spending my evenings alone. We said our farewells with warm group hugs and, particularly from Carolyn, threats and promises to keep in touch. I gave them each an envelope containing a copy of my poem with a request that they wouldn't open them until 5 August – Frances's birthday. That was when I planned to give the poem to my children.

Next day, my friends would start their journey back to Canada via Madrid while I would transfer from my monkish

Pension cell to the majesty of the Parador. For me, at least, the gamut of Camino experiences would continue.

Wandering back to the *Pension*, I thought about my extraordinary outburst in the Pilgrims' office. The farewells to my Canadian friends had helped me begin to understand some of the reasons behind the emotional release I had felt in telling a complete stranger what had driven me along the Camino.

The fact that I had never properly said goodbye to Frances while she was dying had haunted me since her death. When the second brain tumour – the one we had always been told would arise at some point; the one we knew would kill her – manifested itself, Frances seemed to move very quickly into a peaceful, benign state. She showed no curiosity about her condition or circumstances; she seemed totally accepting and unperturbed. She was not in pain and free of any anxiety. I wasn't even sure if she realised she was in hospital and, certainly, when she was moved to the hospice, she appeared not to notice the change in her surroundings.

I became obsessed with the wish to keep her in this calm state: to ensure that she didn't develop enough awareness of her situation to suffer even transitory distress. Frances had survived an astonishing six years since her original diagnosis – a remarkable achievement for someone with a Grade IV glioblastoma. Untreated, death normally followed after a mere

10 or 11 weeks. Fortunately, Frances's first tumour had been operable and, after its removal, she had endured six weeks of intensive radiotherapy followed by chemotherapy. Even so, average survival was still just 12–14 months. In fact, Frances survived so long that, in her final years, she began to suffer adverse consequences caused by her original treatment. She developed post-radiotherapy dementia that affected her short-term memory and cognitive abilities. This was the price she paid for those extra years.

By the time the second tumour showed itself, her short-term memory had become so bad that, even if someone or something had made her aware that she was dying, the realisation and any distress that it caused would have been fleeting. But I wanted to avoid even that.

The consequence was that I felt I had conspired to deny Frances the reality of her death. I had prevented her from somehow understanding it and facing it – from 'owning it', as the current terminology has it. And in doing this, I left myself no opportunity to say my own farewell to her, to acknowledge her as the lodestar of my life and thank her for all the love she had shown me in nearly 43 years together. Part of this, I'm sure, was fear and denial on my part that, after six years we had never expected to be given, the end was finally approaching. It was perhaps me who didn't know how to handle it.

Of course, in her final days Frances was probably beyond communication and comprehension – indeed, the day before she died she seemed to lapse into a coma. By this time, she was at home, in a hospital-style bed installed in our dining room. She had come back home after spending three weeks in the local hospice – far exceeding their 'average stay' of 12 days. In a kindly way it had been made clear that Frances would have to vacate her hospice room at some point – as one of the staff rather bluntly put it: at that stage she wasn't 'actively dying'. In any case, Frances had always expressed a wish to die at home and I was determined to get her back for her 62nd birthday. She came home just four days before it.

Those final 27 days in August were very stressful. Caring for someone you love as death draws inexorably closer is a huge task – one not helped by the fractured nature of the National Health Service in England. It took all my strength to try to comprehend and stay on top of the various branches and agencies that were responsible for different aspects of Frances's care. Some were barely communicating coherently, while others seemed determined to pass the buck to ensure costs were shifted on to someone else's budget. It was a hard, exhausting and emotionally draining time.

Occasionally, bizarre incidents occurred. One day I opened the door to a delivery man who, without a word, handed me a large plastic bag bulging with pharmaceutical items. These turned out to be 'end of life medication': morphine and other drugs and the means to deliver them. Worth a fortune on our local streets, one of the nurses cheerily assured me. But I hadn't known it was coming. No one had thought to warn me.

Just like you never forget the first time a Macmillan cancer care nurse arrives on your doorstep, you will always remember the day a silent courier hands you the means to ease your beloved wife over the threshold of death.

Through it all, Frances remained calm, uncomplaining and pleasant. It was almost as though, in her usual considerate way, she was doing her best to make it as easy as she could for all of us. In the final week she simply stopped eating and drinking and gradually faded away.

On the Thursday morning before her death, it was clear to me that Frances had fallen to a new low ebb. I called our children to tell them it was time to come home. All her family were with her on her last day. And that night, as we slept, Frances slipped peacefully away – selfless and considerate to the end.

Sunday 23 July

Santiago de Compostela

As the *Pension* successfully hid any catering ambitions it might have had, I wandered to a nearby cafe in search of breakfast. The 'complete American' turned out to be eggs, bacon, bread, orange juice and coffee – just what a former pilgrim needed. Throughout my trip the eggs in both Spain and Portugal had been a revelation: vivid orange yolks, luscious whites and almost always served soft and hot from the pan. They had become an almost daily delight.

Much to my disappointment, when I walked through the ornate portal – 'doorway' seemed too humble a word for such a magnificent entrance – of the Hostal dos Reís Católicos, no one challenged this shaggy-bearded, rucksack-toting pilgrim.

At Reception I availed myself of the Parador's stamp to fill the last vacant spot on the page opposite my official Pilgrims' Office endorsements. This pleased me as somehow completing the record of my translation (assumption? Ascension?) from humbler hotels and *pensions* to the hopefully paradisiacal splendours of the Reís Católicos.

Commissioned in 1499 by Ferdinand and Isabella to provide medical care and sustenance for pilgrims arriving in the city, the Hostal remains one of the most splendid buildings in Santiago. Originally, every pilgrim had been entitled to a number of days of rest and recuperation after the rigours of their journey. That role gradually changed over the centuries and the building became a hospital for local people, a function it fulfilled until the 1950s when the last patients were shipped out to a new modern facility. Work then began to convert the building into a five-star Parador which opened in 1954.

My room was on the fourth floor of one of the four quadrangles that form the footprint of the building. I was disappointed to learn that this additional level had simply been plonked on top of the original structure to provide accommodation for hotel guests. So I would be sleeping in 1950s architecture rather than medieval surroundings. While Paradores usually weave modern elements into historic fabric very skilfully, this felt a bit of a let-down.

Nevertheless, the Hostal is a truly astonishing place, though lacking a degree of comfort in that historical heritage clearly takes precedence over soft furnishings. The building feels about 90 per cent national monument and only 10 per cent hotel. No fewer than 79 plaques mark points of interest, forming an historical trail through the establishment. For a time I pursued the recommended trail in an attempt to absorb as much of its history as I could, but also as a way of getting my bearings in this huge and rather baffling building.

Everything about the hotel was monumental. The iconography of the carvings around the main entrance alone would have taken hours to decipher, never mind appreciate.

With morbid fascination I was drawn to the grimly named *Observatorio de Agonizados* – the Observatory of those in the agony of death – on the third floor. A sort of hospice of its day, this was where patients who were about to die were taken so that, as their lives ebbed away, they could hear the singing from the Royal Chapel below. A modest overture, perhaps, to the harmonies of the Seraphim that were sure to follow.

A Latin inscription around the frieze of the cupola above the chapel instructed the reader to: 'Think that death is always threatening us and that our life lasts but an instant. Think how false are delights, how deceptive are honours, how mortal is wealth, how briefly, uncertainly and falsely all this may serve us.

187

Therefore, distance yourself from evil and do good for the poor.'

The words struck a chord with me. Death – and the threat of death – had haunted my childhood. The grim strand of Catholicism in which I was tempered obsessed about mortality. All the hideous elements of death were constantly pored over and rehearsed in graphic detail: the agony of dying (no one, it seemed, ever slipped away with a peaceful passing); the moment of death itself; the immediate aftermath, in which all the petty sins and failings of a lifetime were laid bare as one's soul stood, cowering, before God's judgment; the dread fate that awaited after that baleful tribunal: eternal damnation in Hell, with all the torture and suffering elaborated with sadistic relish, or a few hard years of similar punishment in Purgatory before redemption and admission to the delights of Heaven.

No one, of course, no matter how blameless a life they had led, ever anticipated simply going straight to Heaven. To entertain such a thought, even for a moment, was presumption of the worst kind, worthy of at least a decade of harsh Purgatorial flaying.

Just to pile on the jeopardy, death was capable of deliberate and surprising cunning, designed to catch one unawares. Every night the simple act of going to bed was fraught with terror: the fear of sudden death should God decide to take you when your soul was not in a Persil-pure state of grace but stained, perhaps, by some unabsolved transgression or lewd thought.

Help was at hand, however. Each night, just as we children began to doze off, plops of cold liquid would suddenly shower on to our sleepy heads. Silhouetted in the doorway would be the figure of our Christ-crazed father, shaking holy water over his offspring to keep death and the devil at bay. Nothing could be worse than being snatched, unworthy and unprepared, to face the divine judgement of an angry God. Wet cheeks and a soggy pillow were a small price to pay to avoid such a fate.

Credulous, earnest and compliant I may have been, but I was also an observant and pragmatic child. Thanks to paying close attention at funerals and a vague notion of the effects of *rigor mortis*, I developed my own ingenious method to avoid a premature encounter with the Almighty.

From early childhood I had seen coffins lying before the altar in our chapel, awaiting the funeral Mass and burial service for the deceased. All the coffins, I noticed, were the same, tapering pencil case shape. This struck me as very strange. I knew the body went stiff after death – so how come none of the coffins was ever Y-shaped or star-shaped? Did everyone really die neatly lined up, feet together, hands clasped to allow easy weaving of rosary beads between knarled knuckles? Did no one ever die untidily, spread-eagled all over the bed in the

189

throes of their final excruciating agony? Such a rigid, limb-flung cadaver, I thought, would set the undertaker's carpenter a well-nigh impossible challenge.

Clearly, then, God chose to lie in wait until someone was stretched out, coffin-neat and shroud-ready. Then – zap! – that was it: you've gone to meet your maker. Suddenly I knew how to defeat death. All I had to do to stay alive and sail safely on to morning was spread myself as widely as I could across my bed.

Each night, I would carefully loosen the bedclothes and go to sleep with my arms out of the covers, stretched across either side, and my legs as wide apart as the narrow bed would allow. Now there was no chance of God taking me – not like this. So long as I maintained my untidy starfish splay, I was safe from sudden death.

Every night, after our holy water sluicing, regardless of the chill in the unheated bedroom, I would fling myself into the most freeform posture I could muster and drift off to sleep, happy in the knowledge I had outwitted the Grim Reaper.

And every morning I would wake, horrified to find myself tidily tucked up, arms folded in, and legs aligned in coffin-ready symmetry. Each night I disarranged myself; each morning I woke lying neatly – a sitting duck for a malevolent but perhaps distracted deity, just waiting his chance to pluck me to perdition.

Such was the madness of my upbringing. Who couldn't abhor such a death-obsessed cult? One that saw children go to bed in terror, fear gnawing at young imaginations that should have been filled with playfulness, fantasy and dreams?

Of course, all of this served to make me the easy-going, carefree adult I became! After all, who ever heard of anyone staggering unbalanced out of the miasma of a Catholic childhood?

By way of contrast to the observatory's focus on mortality, more earthly delights were offered on the same floor where the splendid Cardinal's Room came complete with its own hanging balcony. The princes of the church certainly never lacked for comfort. This was where Cardinal Roncalli, then Primate of Venice, stayed in 1954 after he and his host, the Archbishop of Santiago, were the first VIPs to dine in the new Parador's restaurant. Four years later, of course, Cardinal Roncalli became Pope John XXIII.

Also on the third floor, a full set of rooms, still labelled the 'Caudillo's Suite', had been set aside for that murderous old bastard Franco. Given the diminutive dictator's predilection for gruesome capital punishment, I wondered if his quarters offered a garrotting rather than a hanging balcony.

When I felt I had imbibed enough history I headed to the bar, which turned out to be a bleak, functional place with grimly uncomfortable chairs. It didn't invite a long stay, so I followed some more of the history trail but without developing any real passion for the place.

Many of the main function rooms, such as the *Real Comedor* (Royal dining room), were heavily curtained and gloomy, while the Pilgrims' Refectory, which I would have liked to have seen, was firmly locked. This was where, as a nod towards its original function, the hotel still provided a modest free meal for a small number of pilgrims every day.

At the conclusion of their pilgrimage, Hanbury-Tenison recounts the grim experience he and his wife endured when they decided to sample the Parador's traditional pilgrims' fare. Once they had indicated to the hotel staff that they wanted to avail themselves of the free meal privilege, they were brusquely directed out of the hotel, down the side and into the garage. The route led on through a maze of subterranean passages littered with overflowing dustbins and ice-boxes and carpeted with cigarette butts. Their reward was a bowl of noodle soup and a plate of potatoes surmounted by hard-boiled eggs and an indeterminate yellow-orange sauce. This was accompanied by bread, apples and a glass of rosé wine.

The whole experience was clearly utterly dispiriting and carried out in a begrudging and graceless manner at which Hanbury-Tenison rightly took umbrage. I had no idea if the hotel had improved its gratis provision and had no intention of finding out. In any case, I understood one had to apply on the day of arrival with the ink barely dry on one's freshly issued *Compostela*.

Ending my own exploration of the hotel's passages, I settled in the Apothecary's room, a quiet, curtained-off backwater on the first floor, to continue writing out copies of my poem.

In the evening, despite the future Pope's endorsement, I decided not to dine at the Parador but to seek out the San Jaime, the restaurant that had been recommended to me but which we had spurned the previous day.

As instructed, I sat at the bar and ordered a *copa* of their driest albariño. Since crossing into Spain I had noticed that this request invariably led to an exchange in which I would be informed that, in Galicia, albariño was considered not *seco* but sweet. Usually a different Galician wine would be proffered and, to gratify local pride, I always acquiesced and agreed it was fine and truly *seco*.

But not on this occasion. Without demur, a young barman produced a perfectly acceptable albariño and poured it with a flourish. I sipped it slowly, in confident expectation that, as my informant had assured me, a delicious *tapa* would shortly follow.

A local man came in and requested a *copa*. An accompanying *tapa* was immediately supplied. A young couple occupied stools at a small table in the window. A *tapa* arrived with their drinks. Another man sat at the bar beside me and was soon tucking into a *tapa*. This was too much to bear, so finally I exploded to an older man who was innocently washing glasses on the other side of the bar from me.

'No tienes tapa para mi?'

The old guy immediately ordered the young barman to get a *'tapa por señor'*. A lump of warm tortilla and some deep-fried baby squid were produced. Swallowing my sense of grievance at having been overlooked, I fell on them.

As I was mulling over the menu and deciding whether I would have dinner at San Jaime, one of the young servers carried out a large rubbish bin containing a bulging bin liner. He took it outside and then returned behind the bar with the empty bin. The barman who had served me tucked a new bin bag into it. Then both servers carried on doing their jobs without washing their hands.

It reminded me of an episode in the American TV comedy series 'Seinfeld' in which Jerry and his mates have finally secured a table at a fashionable Italian restaurant. He and the guys are in the Gents, eagerly discussing the delights that await them, when the flush goes in one of cubicles.

The amply proportioned chef emerges, greets them warmly, shaking hands all round and promising to make them his personal speciality: a hand-crimped pasta dish. He then exits without washing his hands. Of course, this throws hyper-hygienic Jerry into total panic. He doesn't want to insult the chef or miss out on the kudos of dining at his restaurant, but he can't stomach the idea of eating pasta crimped by hands that emerged unwashed from a toilet stall. What to do?

I couldn't recall the outcome of the episode but I decided I had found my own Seinfeld moment: I had no further need of the San Jaime menu. I wouldn't be eating there. I settled up and moved on down the street, inspecting the tempting seafood and joints of meat displayed in the windows of the many restaurants that lined it.

Nothing makes one hungrier than a single *tapa*. So, still feeling somewhat grumpy, I popped into a busy modern place and walked the length of the bar until I spotted a vacant stool. It was still spinning from the departure of its previous occupant, so I asked the woman sitting alongside if it was free. She assured me it was available.

As usual I requested a dry albariño and, this time, the customary conversation ensued and an alternative wine produced which I was happy to accept. The woman beside me joined in the discussion. She told me her glass of red was very good but she was interested to know what constituted a dry white in Spain. I invited her to taste mine and she declared it more 'brut' than dry. This confused me as I had always thought brut was the driest form of wine. Perhaps she meant the wine was more *brut* than *sec*, as continentals understand it. In any case, she seemed to be a woman of taste.

Clara turned out to be Italian and, by happy chance, a language teacher and keen to practise her English as she was about to lead a group of students from her lyceum on a trip to Eastbourne on the English south coast. She was a bit taken aback but also greatly amused when I told her Eastbourne was one of those seaside towns where the English go to die. She agreed it might not quite meet her students' expectations of a lively English resort.

Clara may have been enjoying her wine but she wasn't happy with the tapas on offer. None of them was spicy enough for her taste – another comment that surprised me, as I hardly associated Italians with spicy food. She opted for a *bomba* and invited me to try one. Sure enough, it proved to be a dull, stodgy lump covered in a slightly piquant sauce.

As I had enjoyed them at the San Jaime, I opted for deep fried squid again. Clara was happy to sample these, but was contrarily unimpressed when I insisted on lacing them with Tabasco.

Despite her objection to my crude chilli addiction, Clara and I seemed to be getting along well. She explained that, after having had a problem with her partner back in Italy, she decided to take herself off to walk the *Camino Portugués* with a friend. Then, for some reason, she and her pal had fallen out and her friend returned to Italy while Clara continued alone. She had loved Portugal and the Portuguese who, we agreed, were friendly and generous people. Our conversation, she told me, was the longest she had had with anyone since starting her solitary Camino. I told her why I had done my Camino and she patted my arm sympathetically.

Eventually, Clara wanted to move outdoors: she needed a cigarette. We settled in a little square further up the street and I ordered two glasses of what was supposed to be Ribera del Duero but which, when it arrived, looked for all the world like Ribena but without the flavour.

Clearly a smoker of the old school, Clara rolled her own cigarettes from a diminishing supply of tobacco, all the time swearing she would give it up once her current pouch was finished. She told me about her 25-year-old son who still lived with her. He had been messaging her frequently during her walk, making it clear it was high time Mama came home to do some washing and, of course, cooking for him. This was par for the course, I understood, for young Italian males.

We soon had enough of Ribena's finest but Clara was keen to have one more drink before ending the evening. We walked up to the cathedral square where I suggested a couple of little bars which lay down some steps below it or, perhaps, my hotel. Clara had been roughing it in *albergues* along the way so, when she discovered I was staying at the Parador, she insisted that's where we should go.

As we approached, she stood astonished, gazing up at the carvings over the entrance. I collected my key and we made our way through the bar and out to the Patio San Marcos, one of the hotel's four internal patios, each named after one of the four evangelists. Here Clara happily resumed puffing, all the time exclaiming at the splendour of the place.

It quickly became clear that Clara had picked up the fortified wine baton from Laurie. At the previous bar she had initially asked for Port but, of course, none was on offer. The Parador's drinks list, however, promised Grahams 10-year-old tawny (as well as Fino, Manzanilla and PX Sherry – Laurie would have to be told) so I ordered a couple of glasses. These went down well, as did the two that followed.

By this point I wasn't sure how the evening would end – or perhaps proceed. I had enjoyed Clara's company and she seemed keen to keep in touch, having given me her contact details.

Clara was some years short of 60 and she had been kind enough to tell me I didn't look 65. With her slightly husky smoker's voice and languid, old hippy manner, she reminded me of a friend back in England. I couldn't honestly decide if I found her intriguing or attractive enough to suggest moving on, perhaps to my room which, at one point, she had inquired about.

But the smoking was a big problem. I really couldn't see myself kissing or getting close to someone who smelled and tasted of cigarettes. And there was also my own fear – of my physicality and attractiveness, and the feeling of not being ready for intimacy, even, perhaps, of a platonic kind after so many years with one person. But perhaps I was getting way ahead of myself: I might have been firmly slapped down for stepping beyond the pleasant brief encounter we had enjoyed.

My dilemma was resolved when Clara needed to return to her *albergue*. After waiting while a brief, surprise shower sprinkled the patio, I walked her to the door where we kissed and said goodnight.

It had been an intriguing encounter. It made me realise that I needed to think through when and how – rather than if – I would be willing to risk intimacy with a new woman. I had felt uneasy and unsure of myself, but that was hardly surprising. This was territory I hadn't ventured into for decades. Forty-two happy years with Frances cast a long shadow – one that I might one day be ready to step out from. But not yet.

It was daunting, but I couldn't help thinking: when was the last time I had walked out of a bar with a woman I had just met? And part of me wondered: had Clara been slightly more my type or at least less thoroughly kippered by her enthusiastic tobacco habit, would I have made a move?

I knew one thing: Frances had told me she didn't want me to be on my own after she had gone. It was still too soon, but one day, perhaps, I might be ready to take her at her word.

Monday 24 July

Santiago de Compostela

After the usual lavish breakfast, I checked out of the Parador with no particular regrets. It would always be one of those places so conscious of its own grandeur that it could never bend enough to embrace you. I had now sampled around 16 of the hotels in the chain, and the Hostal maintained what I had come to think of as a Parador frame of mind. No one ever welcomed you to a Parador. No one said: 'Welcome to Pontevedra' or Tui or wherever. On the contrary, one was often made to feel one's arrival had interrupted important form-filling or box-ticking or whatever pointless procedures the Reception staff felt took priority over new guests. Perhaps a certain initial *froideur* was the price one paid for admittance to what were, after all, nationalised institutions rather than businesses aligned with the more gushing culture of the hospitality sector. Both were objectionable in their way.

The day was far from warm, with lots of threatening cloud. I sat for a time on a bench in the Almeda Park while rain tried unsuccessfully to break through. From the *mirador* I looked across at the monumental cathedral and the buildings around it and understood how overwhelming a sight it must have been for footsore, weary travellers arriving in medieval times.

But my immediate preoccupations were more corporeal. I had become aware that the consequences of a fortnight during which I had paid no attention to my beard or hair were beginning to irk. I looked like the embodiment of one of my own shaggy dog stories. I wanted to find a barber and perhaps buy a new shirt and socks. I had been wearing the same socks for days and swapping between two shirts. It was funny how quickly I had forsaken the Camino laundry habit. But I roamed the streets to no avail: there were no barbers to be found and any shirts I saw were boring and overpriced. I would have to reconcile myself to scruffiness.

In an envelope, I was carrying one of the handwritten copies of my 'Frances Farewell' poem, with a bookmark of photographs of Frances that we had included with the Order of Service at her funeral. I was toying with the idea of secreting these somewhere in the cathedral. I thought Frances would be tickled at the silliness of it. For once, the huge church was relatively empty, with small groups of people wandering aimlessly around. I slipped the envelope behind one of the confessional boxes, smiling at the thought that, at some distant date, someone might find it and be intrigued.

Mission accomplished, I wandered down towards the San Francisco Hotel Monumento, a vast 18th century former monastery tacked on to a huge Franciscan church. After a major renovation the building had reopened in 2005 as a four-star hotel. This was where we had stayed on our 1994 visit, when it was the more modest but still impressive Hogar San Francisco. Then it functioned as part-monastery, part-hotel and I wanted to revisit the former monks' refectory which served as the guests' dining room.

A long, barrel-vaulted room, it had – unlike, I suspected, other parts of the building – survived the renovation with its original features intact. The monks' wooden benches still lined the walls, with a plain stone pulpit jutting out at first floor level from which, no doubt, uplifting spiritual readings were intoned during meals. And, at one end, a huge, dark altarpiece, heavy with carved figures, still presided over the room.

Back in 1994, while we were having dinner there, our younger daughter Hannah, who was then aged nine, went off to find the toilets. After a time, when she hadn't rejoined us, Frances and I set off to look for her. We wandered the adjacent corridors but there was no sign of Hannah until we opened a large door and found her seated happily at the centre of a semi-circle of bearded monks. She had obviously wandered into the monastic part of the building, but seemed totally unperturbed. The scene looked like one of those paintings of 'Christ among the Elders' as Hannah sat giggling amid her fan club of friendly Franciscans. It was clear she and her monkish admirers had been getting along very well.

On my wanderings this time I encountered just one robed monk, so I wasn't sure if any part of the building was still functioning as an active monastery.

After this, I collected my rucksack from the Parador before walking to my billet for the next two nights, the much more modest Hostal dos Estrellas on the Rúa do Pombal. It was certainly a change from the Parador, but perfectly acceptable – clean and modern and clearly the result of a clever architect gutting the original building to maximise accommodation. My room lacked a window on to the street or rear (which looked across at the historic centre and so, not surprisingly, featured strongly on the hostal's website). When he saw my nose pucker at this apparent oversight, my host quickly pointed out that the room still had natural light filtering through a central shaft.

It was the eve of the feast of St James – the most important day of the year in Santiago. I wanted to see how the city was getting ready to celebrate the source of its good fortune. Crowd barriers had been placed in the streets leading up to the cathedral, as well as in the main square itself. Somewhat alarmingly, there was a huge police presence, including fully kitted-out riot squads. The city was prepared for anything and perhaps expecting the worst.

I strolled through the arch past the Archbishop's palace in search of another *tapas* place that had been recommended to me. I found Vinoteca Cervantes and sat up at the bar. Eventually a begrudging *tapa* arrived but I was not impressed. I moved on to a Michelin-recommended restaurant I had picked out as one of the few places that opened on Mondays. It turned out to be a very good choice, staffed by waiters wearing what might have been gay bondage gear: aprons with heavy leather straps and much buckling. They certainly wore their leather with pride and, to be fair, a waitress was kitted out in identical gear.

I had octopus tentacle as a starter. Octopus was a relatively recent enthusiasm of mine and, unrolled on the plate in its full muscular glory, it was a bit intimidating – what my daughter, when she saw a photograph of it later, described as 'a tad anatomical'. But it was perfectly cooked – even the suckers were soft and delicious. Luckily I hadn't yet met the Brummie Camino veteran who described eating octopus as like 'dining on shower mat'!

At the other end of the room, a table of boisterous Americans provided the evening's entertainment. Among their number was an aged, grey-clad nun but the dominant presence was a burly chap in a red shirt who was constantly issuing commands to the waiters. Not content with their responses, he kept yo-yoing up and down to the bar, requesting specific brands of drinks with detailed instructions as to how they should be served.

For all that they happily rove the planet – or at least the 20 per cent of US citizens who have passports, Americans are sometimes the least adventurous of travellers. Many seem to expect – indeed require – that things be served up for them in exactly the same way as back in the good old US of A. This applies particularly to brands of drink and all the accompanying bits and pieces. They seem happy to change the backdrop behind them but not the presentation and content of what they hold in their fists.

This became very clear to me during one of our early trips to Italy. Frances and I were travelling from Venice to Florence when a rockfall in the Apennines brought our train to a juddering halt. We were in the middle of nowhere but, by luck (or design?), just along the track from where the train had stopped was a tiny bar. While the crew worked to clear the line, we climbed down from our carriage and made the most of the opportunity. Among our happy fellow passengers determined to drink the small bar dry, we fell in with a US serviceman, a Master Sergeant in the Military Police, a huge, jovial black man who introduced himself as Big Al.

When it became clear that our train would not reach Florence until the early hours of the morning, Big Al kindly invited us to spend what was left of the night in his apartment in a NATO ammunition base near Pisa. Sure enough, when we eventually pulled into Florence station around 1:30 am, a US Army car complete with armed escort was waiting for him. We happily tagged along and next day, after Al had gone to work, set out to explore our new surroundings.

The base had its own private beach and, as it was high summer, it was full of American teenagers who had joined their parents in Europe for their school or college vacation. It was a hot day and we soon needed a cold drink. That's when we discovered we were no longer in Italy – we were in the United States. The only currency accepted on the base and beach was the US dollar.

We were amazed to learn that everything on the base – milk, bread, vegetables, meat, household goods – was flown in from the States. The PX store – the American equivalent of the British forces NAAFI – was stocked only with directly imported US goods. Everything was organised to replicate Main Street USA.

For all their faults, British forces abroad at least made good use of local suppliers. Their presence, even if unwanted, brought some economic benefit to the host community. The Americans, by contrast, were a sealed sect, their comfort blanket extending from familiar quart cartons of Vitamin D enriched milk to their favourite brands of cookies and toilet paper – all flown in at vast expense to countless US bases around the globe. This was service overseas but with all the familiarity of home.

Back in Santiago, red shirt made another foray to the bar accompanied by one of his fellow diners who was dressed in the robes of a Blackfriar, complete with bulky rosary beads dangling from his belt. They stood for a long time while the friar debated which Jack Daniels or substitute would best suit his needs. It was a scene straight out of Monty Python. Eventually, satisfied with whatever he had procured, the friar returned to the table. I called the head honcho over as he passed and said: 'Put me out of my misery: is the friar for real?'

'You mean the father? Oh, he's for real. You know what we Catholics are like – we love our drink.'

I wasn't sure if I was convinced, but I subsequently noticed another of the males at the table was also in Blackfriar rig. I suppose, if one were ever to see two monks and a nun juggling Jack Daniels at a restaurant table, Santiago de Compostela on the eve of St James's day was a more likely place than most. To add to the theatre, just before the Americans started on their food, the second friar made a great show of saying Grace. Clearly Grace before aperitifs has still to be invented.

After an excellent dinner I headed towards the Cathedral square. I knew a fireworks display was planned to launch the St James's day festivities, but the barriers were now closed and the square totally sealed off. *'Mucha gente'*, a policeman manning one of the blockades explained as he turned me away.

The city was indeed packed. People were perched on viewing points all over the historic centre. On the stage in the Praza da Quitana, where we'd seen the folk group on Saturday, an indie band was just starting up, but I wasn't interested. More or less resigned to watching the fireworks from a distance, I began to drift towards my hotel when I suddenly thought of a ruse to worm my way into the locked-down Cathedral square.

I should have surrendered my Parador guest card when I checked out, but I still had it in my pocket. It showed me as booked in on 23th and out on 24th but I was able to doctor the 24 to make it look like 29. I then presented myself confidently at the next police barrier and, when turned away, explained that I was staying at the Parador. I flashed my card and was allowed to proceed.

The trick held good for the next two barriers and suddenly I was in the teeming central square. As a loyal customer, I felt obliged to stand at the Parador entrance but, after a while, I began to feel uncomfortable. So I insinuated myself past another barrier, without any challenge, to join the throng in the square itself. Everyone was patiently waiting for the fireworks to begin. After a few minutes, I realised I was in an enclosure for disabled and handicapped people and their carers, but, short of developing a limp or trying to be helpful to someone who probably wouldn't appreciate it, there was nothing to be done. I stayed put.

Music played while spotlights and lasers wove dancing patterns of light across the square, up the walls of the cathedral and the palace opposite and into the night sky. At 11:30 the show began. Everyone joined in a countdown to launch a complex light show that was projected across the façade of the Pazo de Raxoi, the seat of local government opposite the cathedral. This was when I realised that the palace wasn't actually undergoing renovation, as I had first thought when I arrived in the city. All the windows across its impressive façade had simply been screened off to facilitate the light show, and the building's roofline, I now noticed, was studded with firework launchers.

After a lengthy display of historical scenes and an account of Santiago's rise to prominence, the lights gave way to the fireworks. These were impressive, sustained and deafening. I was right at the front of the crowd and it was a truly gut-jarring experience. Here were bread and circuses, writ large in colour, noise and explosions across the heavens. And the populace was loving every reverberating moment – blissfully unconcerned about the amount of taxpayers' money being atomised above their heads.

Tuesday 25 July
Saint James's Day

Santiago de Compostela

After breakfast in a café down the street from my hostal, I hung around the rather chilly and windy cathedral square, waiting to see if anything would happen to mark St James's Day. All vestiges of the night before – crowd barriers, launchers from the roof of the palace and all the burnt-out firework debris that had littered the roadway behind it after the previous evening's show – had been cleared away.

The sole remaining barriers were two parallel lines of flimsy airport check-in style tape. These ran from the main door of the palace through the centre of the square to the left of the Archbishop's palace. They indicated that a procession of some sort seemed to be on the cards.

Cheering, flag-waving bands of pilgrims, who had clearly timed their arrival in Santiago to coincide with Saint James's day, began to fill the square. One happy group, all sporting bright red hats with yellow bands, formed a guard of honour for the priests who had led them to this happy conclusion. In dark brown robes and hats with large scallop shells fixed to their fronts, the giggling clerics skipped merrily through a forest of raised walking poles. As if to join in, the sun had come out, the sky was blue and everyone was on a bit of a high.

At noon precisely, a black-suited brass band led a slow parade of dignitaries into the square. There were flag carriers and heralds in colourful tabards; two mace carriers, plenty of sashes and much brass and scrambled egg splashed across the uniforms of representatives of the armed forces and various branches of police. The sharply cut, cardboard-like flat hats that I associated with the Franco era were obviously still in vogue. I assumed the civilians, some wearing chains of office, were members of local or regional councils. Soldiers in magnificent 18th century uniforms, complete with plumed helmets, cavalry boots and swords, brought up the rear. The whole thing was a carnival collision of civic pomp and operetta. A *zarzuela* for Saint James.

And, suddenly, that was it. The dignitaries disappeared into the palace, presumably for a reception before lunch, and the square quickly returned to normal. I was surprised by the total absence of clergy in the parade. Perhaps the ecclesiastical forces who had flocked to the city for its annual big day had more important things to do, such as fire up the *botafumeiro* for the saint's day High Mass in the cathedral. I knew it would be swinging in honour of Saint James but that wasn't enough to persuade me to sit through another lengthy ceremony – even if I could have got in.

The day continued to warm up as I wandered the streets taking note – really for the first time – of the number of buildings that boasted pillars, pilasters, detailed classical ornamentation, huge coats of arms and statues of *Santiago Matamoros* (St James, slayer of moors) and other ecclesiastical notables. The university, in particular, had a fine showing of monumental faculty buildings. Here was a city with a strong sense of its own importance.

I was enjoying a light lunch of beer and nibbles at Cervantes Vinoteca when I was joined by a chatty Brummie couple. Having finished the *Camino Francés* a week ahead of schedule, the husband had jumped on a train to Ferrol and followed up by walking the *Camino Ingles*. The Camino to which the English give their name starts on the north coast of Galicia, where pilgrims would arrive by sea, and is around 120 kilometres – just slightly more than the minimum distance required to earn a *Compostela*. Fair play to the sensible English – they were never inclined to push the envelope when it came to pious exertion.

But the word on the street was that the English were approaching from another direction. According to my Brummie informant, a pre-production BBC TV crew had been spotted scouting locations along the *Camino Francés*. This was for a proposed reality TV series in which a group of minor celebrities would be filmed walking the Camino and no doubt giving us the benefit of their inner journey and spiritual struggles. That was just what Santiago's field of stars needed – a sprinkling of the dubious fairy dust of reality TV.

The indefatigable Brummie and his wife were now planning to walk the westward Camino from Santiago to the coast at Finisterre, the fabled 'end of the world'. This is the only Camino that actually begins in Santiago and it has ancient pagan associations as well as more recent Christian overtones. Many hardened hikers liked to finish their Camino immersion by continuing to the lighthouse at Finisterre. Watching the sun set into the ocean provided a fitting finale to the experience. As this would be her first attempt at a Camino, however, the wife was apprehensive, but her husband had clearly got the pilgrim bug big time. Nothing was going to stop him completing his hat-trick of Caminos.

My immediate plans were rather more indulgent. I hoped to round off the privations and mortification of my pilgrimage by eating my last supper at Casa Marcelo, a popular Michelin-starred restaurant just down from the Parador. It didn't take bookings for parties of fewer than eight, so the trick was to turn up just as they opened at 8:30 and hopefully pile in.

In preparation, I installed myself on the pavement outside a bar on the Rua das Hortas, just round the corner from the restaurant. The only slight drawback was that I couldn't actually keep watch in case a substantial queue formed. I would have to take my chances. I had a final 'dry' exchange with the charming young waitress and happily accepted her vinous recommendation, once again spurning 'sweet' albariño.

For want of anything better to do, I found myself eavesdropping on a tedious, circular conversation at the next table, involving two Englishmen and a Spanish woman. The lead talker, a convinced Christian, was extolling the rewards of something called the Alpha course to his fellow countryman. A few years back I had noticed a rash of promotion posters for this course in England. It seemed to be aimed particularly at young people struggling to make their way in London and other big cities, but I knew nothing else about it.

The course had clearly paid dividends for the speaker, as he was keen to enumerate in some detail. It had given new meaning to his life. It had brought him great blessings and shown him that God loved him more than anyone else in the world. Clearly not totally won over, his counterpart voiced tentative but 'deeply respectful' scepticism, while the soft-spoken Spanish lady danced a diplomatic fandango between the two.

It was a repetitive and deeply boring exchange but it made me realise that it was the first actual religious wrangling I had encountered during two weeks on the Camino. Thank God for that. Long may the sceptics carry on hiking.

Around 8:25 I thought I'd better head to the restaurant and, on turning the corner, I was dismayed to see that quite a crowd was huddled round Marcelo's still firmly closed door. There was, of course, nothing so formal or organised as a queue.

I fell in behind a cheery bunch of Italians who told me they had been advised by their taxi driver to try Marcelo's. They had just walked the entire *Camino Portugués* from Lisbon and, like me, this was their last night in Santiago. They were determined to seal their pilgrimage with an indulgent evening of adventurous cooking.

As soon as the door opened, a group of about eight people dashed straight to an area beyond the open cooking station. A few more set themselves up at the bar opposite the chefs where they could watch the dishes being prepared. The Italians perched themselves on stools either side of a long, central communal table that could accommodate about 22 people. I noticed that disposable wooden cutlery was jammed into mugs in the centre of the tables. This was clearly an informal sort of place.

I was dithering as to where I should sit when the Italians insisted that I join them. Most couldn't speak English and what little Italian I once possessed had withered to almost nothing, but one of the quieter members of the party – a retired pharmacist – took me under her wing and we got through the evening pretty well.

A confident young chef, who may or may not have been Marcelo, came over to check for allergies or anything we wouldn't eat. Just one woman confessed to the sin of vegetarianism, otherwise we were game for anything. There was no menu but our host promised an eclectic mix of Galician, Peruvian and Japanese cuisine. It sounded promising. We simply had to surrender to the whims of our patron who guaranteed us a series of dishes he was sure everyone would enjoy.

By this time the room had filled up and there was an air of enthusiastic anticipation, helped along by the laughter and exuberance of my Italian friends. Sitting across from me were a mother and daughter from Wexford. They were, I suddenly realised, the first Irish people I had met since saying goodbye to my siblings in Porto.

Dishes arrived in rapid succession. All were colourful and many were presented with a theatrical flourish. Some were served in individual portions while other dishes were for sharing. One of the latter was an astonishing deep fried red snapper or gurnard that sat, crisp and golden, in open-mouthed astonishment at its fate, on a wooden board for four of us to demolish.

We started with a refreshing melon mojito then moved on to a colourful and tangy combination of red peppers, tomatoes and cheese. A play on the Ulster fry that featured potatoes, bacon and eggs certainly hit a familiar warm spot with me, while a mackerel fillet arrived, exuding smoke through a hole in the top of the perfectly formed cloche of crusty bread that hid it. Capon cannelloni was rather spoiled by a slimy noodle-style accompaniment, but the passion fruit sorbet that followed was superb.

It was a light, playful meal that tickled our visual senses as much as our taste buds. After eight or so seductive courses, the feeling of indulgent guilt among my fellow diners was such that we resolved, one day, to undertake another Camino simply to redeem ourselves.

After a very enjoyable evening I said goodbye to my lively Italian friends and climbed the steps to the *Praza do Obradoiro* for the last time.

Darkness had fallen over the city. The swaddled, black bulk of the cathedral's great western front etched itself against a melancholy sky. The huge square was quiet and deserted: all the daytime beggars, living statues and celebrating pilgrims had gone. The silence was in marked contrast to the explosions of the previous night.

Finale

It was time to say goodbye to Santiago. In the 23 years since my first visit, the city had changed immensely. The pilgrim trade had revived beyond the wildest dreams of the city fathers. Santiago was now firmly established as a global destination, with young and old literally beating a path to its medieval portals which were flung wide to greet them. According to the Confraternity of St James, in 1994 when I had first visited the city, fewer than 16,000 pilgrims received a *Compostela*. By the end of 2017, for the first time more than 300,000 pilgrims would stumble into the cathedral square. People were already talking about having hit 'peak Camino'. On top of that, thousands more arrived by car or plane simply as tourists.

Inevitably, the city had become more brashly commercial and perhaps just a tad greedy. All its very public spirituality had its counterpart in brash materialism: tourist tat was everywhere. Yet there was still much about the place that appealed: the music, seafood, architecture and cultural life. Above all, there was the pride of the people of Galicia in their region, language and heritage.

One could not help but admire the sheer guts involved in keeping this frequently sodden city not just afloat but important and vibrant. Here was a community sustaining a 21st century economy on blister pads, scallop shells and the enduring myth of an apostle's bones found in a field of stars. It was an unlikely recipe for civic success – but it worked.

Whatever the hopes, the dreams, the sadness, confusion, grief, belief, disbelief or distraction that drew this throbbing, aching, sweaty stream of humanity to this proud city, something in the air in Santiago clearly resonated and perhaps occasionally provided the echo of a response.

For my part, my pilgrimage – if that's what it had been – was over. Tomorrow I would return to England to resume my new life: learning how to live as a widower. The Camino had helped me realise that I probably would find a way to thrive as an individual rather than the relict half of a couple. It had shown me friendship and companionship and rekindled an openness to the kindness of strangers. I had been reassured about my capacity for sociability. If I became a crank or a recluse, it would be my own choice. But, with a grandchild on the way, there was the promise of new life – another generation, but one that would grow up with the sad absence of someone who would have been for them a wonderful grandmother.

I thought back to a night in the 1970s when Frances and I popped into a tiny dancehall in a remote part of Donegal. As in all the dancehalls of my youth, the girls were lined up along one side of the room, doing their best to look haughty, indifferent and composed. Opposite them was a wall of sheepish lads, risking furtive glances from beneath brooding Celtic eyebrows. To all intents and purposes this seemed an unbridgeable divide. Then the music started. The lads swept across the floor to grab a partner. Instantly the hall became a swirl of spinning bodies. Though almost half a century lay behind me since that Donegal night, I knew it would soon be time for me to hit the floor again and re-enter the dance of life.

I turned back, crossed the empty square and headed down the steps. A soft breeze wafted up from the lower town. It brushed against my cheeks with the promise of warmth to come. And, gently, on the displaced air, perhaps I could just hear Frances whispering: 'Go on'.

EPILOGUE I
Poems for Frances

Stones In Our Pathway

I brought you a stone from the Camino
And one from the West Highland Way.
I laid them in Warblington graveyard,
In the place where we left you that day.

And if ever I circuit the Balkans
Or wander west Kerry's wild hills,
I'll look out for basalt or granite,
For limestone with ammonite frills.

For you're not just in Warblington graveyard,
You've paced Santiago with me;
I followed your shadow to Rannoch
And on past the Devil's rough scree.

So I'll keep bringing stones from my travels,
Build a path from your head to your foot;
And we'll walk from Fort William to Dingle,
Here – where our once longed-for future took root.

Parting II

A cloudless September day,
Vivid blue sky bathing
The head of the harbour.
Within a maelstrom of people
I spin through hugs and kisses
And handshakes from family and friends
Stirring a warm broth of kindness.

Later, opening the car, our children
Accounted for, I look round for you.
The instinct of forty years tells me
You will be woven into a knot
Of merriment and laughter,
Your open, smiling face, as ever,
At the heart of the throng.

And then it hits me:
You're not coming with us.
We are leaving you behind,
In your wicker cage and
Narrow, mud-dark cell.
The grey funeral car thrums,
Droning undertone of farewell.

Warblington
8 September 2016

Grave Matters

We almost bought two graves today,
Just off the Crewkerne road.
Sign: 'Natural Burial Site',
You sensed a neat abode.

A soft breast of verdant hillside
Where sheep may safely graze,
Sweeping views to far-off Stourhead
And Somerset ablaze.

A pleasant, helpful farmer's wife
Explained all that it took.
'Diversifying our pasture.
Just sign here in the book.'

Seriously we took the task
And trod her acres wide.
We picked a spot where we could be
Through ages side by side.

But back home we lost our mettle
And kept the chequebook shut.
There'll be another day, we said,
To dig our compost rut.

We almost bought two graves today,
In Dorset, Hardy's loam.
A darkling thrush sang overhead:
Our final English home.

Grammar Lesson

My father always spoke about 'My house',
A phrase that grated on your ears.
We flourished in the realm of 'our',
A shared community – equal, joint,
Generously enfolding us and ours.
But now I've slipped from 'our' to 'my',
Eliding to a linguistic landscape
Unoccupied for more than forty years.
Learning my part from partnership,
I parse my present warily in a stand
Of solitary 'I's. In the land of the selfie,
I hold at arm's length my possessive alone.

Pillow Talk

Tomorrow I must buy a bolster
To spread cross our bed's riven head.
Then I'll slyly roll into the middle
And accept you're not sleeping – you're dead.

Touchstones

I

Quitting the Dordogne sunshine,
The rackety little train
Draws us into the earth.
Shadows flittering, time stretching,
On to the depths of the cave.
Around and above, long-dead hands
Semaphore greeting and farewell.
Through lines of lumbering bison
Soft finger-flutings of
Darkness-defying children
Rope us to the past.

II

Beaming, fulfilled, you come
From the back room;
A vivid morning spent
Stabbing colour into canvas,
Palette-knifing the sky.
Gripping both handrails
You struggle downstairs,
Balance hanging on every step.
Bangles scrabble chalky emulsion;
Oily smudges from hand
Or sleeve scumble the wall.

III

Long after you've gone
These spoors remain,
Pulses of presence
On your Calvary trail.
One day, perhaps, I will
Repaint the stairwell,
But, for now, I follow
Your Rouffignac train;
Brushing the wall
I descend, briefly again
Hand-in-hand with you.

EPILOGUE II

Poems by Frances Hamblin

For Maeve, Hannah, Conor
whom Frances loved beyond words

First published by Paekakariki Press in 2018
in a limited edition for private circulation
All rights reserved
© The Estate of Frances Hamblin 2018

239

Editor's note

In June 2010 my wife, Frances Hamblin, was diagnosed with a glioblastoma grade IV – the most aggressive form of brain tumour. A previously fit and healthy woman, Frances now faced the grim reality of a life-limiting illness, with average life expectancy of 12–14 months even after treatment. Following the diagnosis, Frances began to keep a journal and continued writing on an almost daily basis until two months before her death. In January 2018 I read these journals for the first time and found scattered within them all but one of the poems I have brought together in this collection.

These poems were clearly written spontaneously, with little attempt at artifice or revision and, almost certainly, no notion of publication. The exception is the final poem, 'I Am Not', which Frances wrote in 2009 for the funeral of her beloved father, Tom. This poem was also used to close her own funeral service following her death on 27 August 2016, aged 62.

This collection was previously published in 2018 in a limited edition printed by the Paekakariki Press, Walthamstow. I have included them in this book as a way of bringing them to the attention of a wider audience.

Frances was modest and self-deprecating about her many creative talents. These poignant and honest poems preserve aspects of her distinctive voice – her humour, sensibility and concern for others; her courage in the face of fate.

Echoes of a warm and generous spirit, they deserve to be heard.

PATRICK TIERNEY

Star Travelling

Salt tears, my face streaming,
Talking and saying and voicing.
Remembering the places you'd been,
The good times you'd had;
Where you'd been happiest, your children
And grandchildren, the warm sun on your face,
The wonderful woman you are. How I love you.

Holding your shoulders, trying to support your weight
As you lay back and your eyes rolled briefly.
Pleading with you to stay with us and your arms
Reaching, reaching up; your hands like claws
Grasping up, up they went. Your eyes up into
The depths of their sockets. Up to the stars you went,
Up, up. Who could not think of heaven or a better place
Than the one you'd left – star traveller mum.

Steroid Sisters

for Geraldine and Maria

Separated by the old third world
Three moon-faced women wait –
Perfumed and maquillaged –
While, tight-girdled in between,
Teem and sweat the rest.
A heavy, close-embroidered,
Three-cornered mantle
Yokes the three together
To frustrate fate.

The Silver Birch

A brilliant spring sun has polished
The bright silver needle of the birch trunk.
It gleams as it pierces the cobalt velvet backdrop
To the universe and gently shakes its head.
The blond-tipped auburn tresses of its branches
Weave and sway, seduction of the hour.

Mantequilla

Mantequilla,
Such a beautiful word.
The first Spanish word
That Hannah learned
And, as it means butter,
One of my favourites to utter too,
And Hannah's favourite to mutter
Or stutter or splutter,
Laughing with a mouthful of bread and butter,
Adding to the mess and clutter
On the family breakfast table.

Sandbanks, August 2011

It matters little when you're dead
Whom you've met or what you said.
There'll be no calling to call out
Because you're sick and so not fit
For the scrutiny of it.
No one will heed that while they wept
For you, you slept.

The sun crept down the western sky
And blasted the Isle of Wight into sight.
Its chalk cliffs on the edge, upright
To the flat horizon of the sea.
And I awoke and they said how beautifully
I'd slept, how still and quiet and calm.
I thought: 'I'm practising for the grave'
And knew they'd seen me then
As on a bier forewarned.

Winter Reflections

A brilliant yellow-sun winter morning
Bright with puddles.
Inverted twigs of trees,
Smudges of bright cloud
And slants of golden light
Pave my way today.

Fucking February

Fucking February, with its two 'r's.
Here we are at last, drawing towards one 'r',
The arse end of February.
I always hated you with your mean, thin
Winter light; cold-hearted, miskeen air,
Threaded with fog; your drizzling, mizzling dampness
And streaky condensation trailing evil black damp
On every window frame.

February hangs heavy like a yoke on old shoulders.
Arthriticky, the pails barely swing. No joyful rattle
Of a job well done; just the threat of more of the same
Tomorrow.

Thank God you're only 28 days long –
But 29 in each leap year.
February in England: wish that March were here.

Southsea
February 2011

Little Mote Song

See the motes go floating by,
Even though they're in my eye
I believe they're in the sky.
When I see them whizzing now,
Little bits of nothing much,
Circles in the blue beyond,
Though I know they're in my eye
And can't be caught or smelled or touched,
I still believe they're in the sky
And not just in my little eye.

Titanium Screws Blues

Titanium screws, titanium screws,
I've got the titanium screws blues.
When they rejoin your skull
What do they use?
Titanium screws, titanium screws.

They bevel the edges so it goes in neat,
Bone on bone; not meat on meat.
And they screw it in place
And what do they use?
Titanium screws, titanium screws.

There's a lifetime guarantee
On those titanium screws,
But that's no solace for
The titanium screws blues.
Those screw heads are felt

As bumps in the night,
Lumps under my scalp,
Tender and tight.
Titanium screws, titanium screws.
I've got the titanium screws blues.

25 June 2011

Let Me Go And The Music Will Flow

for Stephanie from Kate

In the mists of the dream world a shadow crept,
Becoming distinguishable as a child
With luminous skin and a light within,
Her outstretched hand waiting to be caught up.

You reach out to take the hand and grip –
Nothing, thin air. That's when you wept.
You know this child. She looks up and says simply:
'Please let me go. Then you too can be free
And your music will flow more easily.'

I Don't Cry

A mother's lament

I don't cry because I know I'm going to die,
But for the life I'll miss,
Every hug and kiss,
And the turning world I'm not ready to leave,
And the pain of darling children
And sweet husband left to grieve.

If only I could have spared you this
(And, in sparing you, I would myself be saved
And the Fates deceived).
But that would have been to turn time on its head
Or to rub a Genie's lamp and be granted
An ungrantable wish,
Spurning death's tread
And refusing
The severed thread.

1 June 2011

What Do I Wish For You?

Every snapped wishbone and shooting star,
Every white horse and magpie pair,
I make a wish for you too.
What do I wish for you?

Number one, good health.
Secondly, adequate wealth.
Then enough good books to read
And the eyesight you'll need
To read them. The ingredients
To cook a fancy dish;
The nous to learn a new skill: to fish
Or speak Turkish:
'*Teşekkür ederim*'.

I wish that your great grandchildren
Will know you; will know the kind,
Thoughtful, funny man you are
And how lucky they'll think me
For a lifetime with you.

I wish that you'll keep
Your own hair and teeth,
And that death, when it comes,
Will be like stealth in the night
As you sleep, not waking before
Slipping away.

What else do I wish you?
Whatever you wish yourself.
May it be yours.

Andalucia
November 2011

Little Poem To My Grandchildren

Three score years and ten –
That's all I'd need and, by then,
My children may have had children of their own
And I would be a grandma they had known,
Not just a photo or a snatch of film,
But a living, breathing, cuddling human being.

13 March 2011

I Am Not

I am not.
Not ash, not bone,
No voice, no further care.
I am no one, nowhere.
I am the gap I leave,
Displacing no air.

Biographical note

Frances Lynnette Hamblin was born in London on 5 August 1954. After a childhood spent in England, Somaliland, Malta and Cyprus, she studied philosophy at Queen's University Belfast.

Moving to Portsmouth in 1978, Frances trained as a teacher to pursue her passionate belief in the capacity of education to transform difficult and disadvantaged lives.

After teaching children with educational and behavioural problems, Frances worked with adults with learning and physical disabilities and with many people for whom English was a second language. She developed a particular interest in deaf and dyslexic students and pursued this subject area by gaining an MSc from the University of Southampton in phonological processing.

An active trade unionist, Frances helped combat a climate of bullying at the University of Portsmouth, where she became a senior lecturer in the Academic Skills Unit. She served on a number of university committees and, when she retired due to ill health in 2011, her contribution towards changing the culture of the organisation was acknowledged.

In April 1979 Frances married Patrick Tierney. The couple had three children: Maeve, Hannah and Conor. A wonderful wife and mother, Frances pursued myriad active and creative interests with her wide circles of friends. Her novel 'Warehouse' was published in 2014.

Frances died at home in Southsea on 27 August 2016.

Acknowledgements

I am grateful to many people who encouraged me to write this book. In the first place to the friend whose queries, while considering a hike along part of the *Camino Portugués*, caused me to revisit the notebooks I had kept during my walk. Having read them, I decided to type them up with the intention of perhaps at least sharing my account with my children. Subsequently, a number of family members and friends to whom I showed my Camino ramblings very kindly urged me to make them more widely available. Whether that was a sensible response I will leave to the good sense of you, the reader.

To spare their blushes I have changed the names of some of my fellow pilgrims and hikers. I hope I have not been unduly unkind to any of them but, in any case, I would like to express my sincere thanks to all those who travelled with me and befriended me along the way.

My gratitude goes in particular to Carolyn and Laurie for their open-hearted fellowship and for being such good company. I will be forever grateful that, on my second day on the Camino, our paths so fortuitously crossed in the cool stillness of the Romanesque church in Rates.

I am also indebted to my friends the Jahoda family for allowing me to interrupt their holiday in Portugal and for their warm welcome and unstinting hospitality. Utterly predictable, of course, but never taken for granted.

Based on their own experience walking the *Camino Francés*, my good friends Mark Newman and Lesley-Anne Knight were sources of sound advice on equipment, clothing and many other matters. Their example and encouragement were key factors in setting me on my way.

Like countless Camino hikers before me I am indebted to the work of John Brierley, author of numerous guides to all the various paths that lead to Santiago. His regularly updated *'Pilgrim's Guide to the Camino Portugués'* is an invaluable source of helpful detail on the vagaries of the route, accommodation and dining options along the way, as well as the physical nature of the terrain and the history all around.

ACKNOWLEDGEMENTS

My thanks go to my former colleagues Chris Stone of Stone Creative for his meticulous assistance in preparing the book for print and to James Holt of Version One for producing the cover.

I have been touched by the concern my children – Maeve, Hannah and Conor – have shown me since they suffered the immeasurable loss of their mother. They have frequently urged me to write something of my experiences. Now that I have done so, I hope these further revelations of their father's foibles and limitations will not lower me too much in their regard.

My grandsons, Dominic Francis Forster and Rafferty Francis Earnshaw, who entered our lives after Frances's death, are beaming pilot lights drawing me onward to the future.

Finally, I can never possibly attempt to measure the debt I owe to the woman who shared so much of her life's journey with me. Having Frances at my side for almost 43 years was the greatest gift of my life. Her presence in these pages is a pale reflection of the light she cast when she moved so vividly among us. Its warmth continues even as its gleam fades.

PATRICK TIERNEY

Southsea

June 2020

northwardtosantiago@gmail.com

CERTIFICACIÓN DE PASO (sellos)

las casillas deberá figurar el sello de cada localidad (al menos 2 por día)
con la fecha, para acreditar su paso

PARADOR DE PONTEVEDRA

Fecha 18/07/2017

19/7/2017

Descanso del Peregrino

Fecha Máquinas expendedoras
35259718-M

O Cuberto
Angel Manuel Outeymino Buxal
76269030-Y
Arcos de Condesa
Caldas de Reis

Fecha 19/7/2017

BALNEARIO ACUÑA

T. 986 540 010
CALDAS DE REIS

Fecha

PROTECCIÓN CIVIL · CONCELLO DE VALGA
20 XULL. 2017

Fecha

Fecha 19/07/17

SAN MIGUEL
CAMIÑO PORTUGUÉS
Telf. 986 - 559131

Pensión R. Jardín

Fecha 20/7/2017

Fecha

20-07-17

CERTIFICACIÓN DE PASO (sellos)

En las casillas deberá figurar el sello de cada localidad (al menos 2 por día)
con la fecha, para acreditar su paso

PARROQUIA DE SANTIAGO DE PADRÓN
CAMINO DE SANTIAGO
ARZOBISPADO DE SANTIAGO

Fecha ___ ___ 2017

A CASA DOS MARTÍNEZ
CIF: E - 15781867
rúa longa, 7 - 15900 Padrón
Telf.: 634 980 536

Fecha 20 . 7 . 2017

SANTUARIO DE NUESTRA SEÑORA DE LA ESCRAVITUD

Fecha 22 . 7 . 2017

25 / 7 / 2017

CRUCEIRO DE FRANCOS
CAMINO PORTUGUÉS

PARADA DE FRANCOS
CASA RURAL RESTAURANTE
981 538004

Fecha 21 / 07 / 2017

Fecha

Hospital G. ... desde 1499
PARADORES

BAR DESCANSO
do PEREGRINO
AS GALANAS - TEO (A CORUÑA)

Fecha 22 - 07 - 17

Fecha

CERTIFICACIÓN DE PASO (sellos)

En las casillas deberá figurar el **sello de cada localidad (al menos 2 por día)** con la **fecha**, para acreditar su paso

Fecha   Fecha

2 2 JUL. 2017

Fecha   Fecha

Fecha

2 2 JUL. 2017

Fecha   Fecha

Printed in Poland
by Amazon Fulfillment
Poland Sp. z o.o., Wrocław

60109147R00164